PARANORMAL INVESTIGATO ...ION
BOOKS 1 - 10

First edition. September 22, 2017.

Written by rodney cannon.

To all of the paranormal investigators past and future. You guys and gals do not get the respect that you deserve.

PARANORMAL INVESTIGATORS - COMPLETE COLLECTION - BOOKS 1 - 10

By.

Rodney C. Cannon and Leo Hardy

BOOK ONE

Paranormal Investigators One

Ed and Lorraine Warren, The Enfield Poltergeist

Chapter One Between Movies and Reality

"Diabolical forces are formidable. These forces are eternal, and they exist today. The fairy tale is true. The devil exists. God exists. And for us, as people, our very destiny hinges upon which one we elect to follow." — *Ed Warren*

I arrived here almost the same way that most of you did. We saw a movie and we wanted to know more about the couple that inspired it. Before we really get started I would like to tell you a little something about myself. My background is as a screenwriter and as a micro budget filmmaker. I have harbored a love of stories about the supernatural since I was a child. It dates not only back to the movies that I saw as a child, but some encounters with the supernatural. Some would argue that whatever I heard or saw was the imagination of a small child, but most of those experiences were shared with other children in my family and even decades later we remember the events the same.

This book is not written to convince you about the existence of the supernatural either you believe or you do not. Just understand that before I begin that I believe in both good and evil. I believe in heaven and hell. I believe that not only people, but other things wander through our realm of existence and some of those other things mean us harm. If you need to place it in a more scientific context then I suppose that you can look at god and angels as positive forces and the devil, demons and evil itself as negative forces. Just as neutrons and electrons oppose each other.

This book is a short one for a reason. I wanted to touch upon a story and a few of the people involved. If you want to read the whole story you will find that Ed and Lorraine have written many books that focus on some of their more interesting cases. Also keep in mind that movies, no matter how well made, offer only a glimpse at the truth behind the events.

If you like this book, please remember to mention it to a friend and to leave a review. Thank you and god bless you.

Chapter Two Human Spirits and Evil Spirits

In the world of the paranormal, hauntings are very common occurrences. Individuals or families who have never before had any type of paranormal encounter - some who didn't even believe in such things - have suddenly found themselves the victims of terrifying ordeals brought about by dark spiritual forces.

Paranormal experts classify hauntings into two basic categories: human, or "ghost" hauntings, and demonic hauntings, generally those of a more sinister nature. Ghost hauntings are quite common. They are referred to as human hauntings because the common belief is that ghosts are the spirits of those who have died and who, for whatever reason, remain in the earthly realm. No one knows whether this is in fact what ghosts are, or if so why some of them choose to frighten and attack the living sometimes. It is possible that ghosts don't know they have passed on or they were not ready to go yet, so they remain earthbound as long as they can. Another possibility is that they may have unfinished business here and want to communicate this to someone still in the world of the living. It is quite possible that for the most part ghosts don't mean to frighten the living, but by their very nature, it happens. Still others may choose to haunt the living, enjoying the fear they instill. At this point there is simply no evidence as to why ghosts exist, what they are, and why they haunt the living.

Demonic hauntings on the other hand are identifiable by their vicious, evil, and harmful nature. The entities in these types of hauntings often hit, bite, scratch, burn, pinch, slap, or otherwise do physical harm to the victim. Whereas in ghostly hauntings the activities of the spirit are usually done surreptitiously and are rarely physically harmful, demonic hauntings can include victims being made physically ill, experiencing actual symptoms such as fever, vomiting, seizures, heart problems, fatigue, headaches, all unexplainable by medical means. A ghostly haunting can occur for rather benign reasons; demonic hauntings are never so. They occur with a sole purpose, and that is to harm or destroy the lives of the victims.

To date there is no scientific proof of either type of haunting, or the existence of a spirit world at all. However, for those who study these types of occurrences, and especially for those who have encountered them, there is no doubt that the spirit realm is very real and very active in the world of the living.

CHAPTER THREE Spirit Boards more risk Than Reward

"Why do so few 'scientists' ever look at the evidence for telepathy, so called? Because they think, as a leading biologist, now dead, once said to me, that even if such a thing were true, scientists ought to band together to keep it suppressed and concealed. It would undo the uniformity of nature and all sorts of other things without which scientists cannot carry on their pursuits. . . ." — Ed Warren, Graveyard

The spirit board, also known as the Ouija board, has been popularly used since the time it was introduced on the commercial market in 1890 by a man named Elijah Bond. It has actually existed since ancient times in various forms. As far back as 540 B.C, mystic tables that were set on wheels were used in séances to contact dead spirits.

Elijah Bond marketed the board as a parlor game. According to some historians, when Mr. Bond attempted to get the patent for the game, the patent officer told him that he would first have to prove that it worked by having it spell out his own name, which was unknown to anyone in the room. When it did, the astonished officer gave him the patent.

The use of the board took off during the Great Depression, when it was used as a form of mystical family entertainment. It was also commonly used by spiritualists as a way to contact the dead and receive guidance. Today the Ouija board is seen as a harmless game that is even played by children. But is it harmless?

The Hidden Reality Behind the Spirit Board.

The use of spirit boards is actually a form of witchcraft. Whether or not the user is an innocent participant or an intentional diviner of spirits is unimportant. The same dark forces, evil spirits and demons are at work regardless.

An easy way to understand this is when a young child strikes a match. He may be unaware at the time of the power of what he has just done, but he is likely to get burned anyway. The spirit board is a portal or doorway into the world of the occult, where unseen dark forces are at work.

Witchcraft as a practice is condemned in the Bible, as seen in Deuteronomy 18, which lists several occult practices, including consulting with familiar spirits. To understand why, you must understand the nature of God, and the nature of the devil.

God and The Devil

We all know that God is the epitome of love. God created man because He loved him, but as early as creation the devil appeared, seeking to tempt man to disbelieve and disobey God. The devil is variously described in the Bible as a deceiver, one who tempts man to sin against God, one who causes turmoil and confusion, and even death.

Jesus gave a very clear definition of the purposes of God and the purposes of the devil, whom he called the thief. He said, "The thief comes only to steal and kill and destroy; I have come that they may have life, and have it to the full. (John 10:10, NIV)

It is important to realize that the devil will try to harm you if he can. He doesn't care whether you believe he exists or not.

What God asks of man in return for His love, care and protection is man's allegiance only to Him, as evidenced by the First Commandment. Witchcraft is condemned in the Bible because it seeks to obtain guidance not from God, but from other supernatural forces in the unseen world.

You do not have to try to contact a ghost in order to obtain guidance for your life. God has all the guidance you will ever need. All you have to do is call upon Him in prayer.

Avoid using such items as spirit boards or you may invite dangerous forces into your home and your life. The story of the Hodgson family is a case that should give all of us pause.

CHAPTER FOUR THE HODGSON FAMILY

"Mediums and spiritualists invoke powerful spirits or the souls of the dead, without realizing that they have given themselves body and soul to demonic powers. Even if it is not immediately evident, those powerful spirits always use their minions for destructive purposes.-

Gabriele Amorth Exorcist

The Hodgson family was made up of Peggy Hodgson and her four children two of which experienced what was deemed as poltergeist activity. Peggy called the police and claimed furniture had moved around the room unattended and that her daughters had been scared by ghostly sounds. Margaret, age 13, and her sister Janet, age 11, claimed they had seen and heard a ghost. They claimed they had been levitated around the room. Their story was found to be fraudulent by some who had discovered Janet banging a broomstick against the ceiling and hiding a tape recorder to give the illusion of poltergeist activity.

Later demonic voices had been heard in the neighborhood. Rocks and toys had been reported flying around outside. Overturned chairs and children suspended in midair had been reported. The story was covered in British newspapers the Daily Mail and the Daily Mirror.

On Halloween 2011, BBC News showed an interview with Graham Morris, a photographer, who claimed the events from 1977 were genuine.

Grosse and Playfair were two researchers who were members of the Society for Psychical Research that claimed the haunted house to be genuine. When Janet and Margaret admitted to their tricks to the reporters of the day, Playfair and Grosse convinced them to retract their revelations and hold to the original story. Janet had been accused of being a ventriloquist when strange voices were heard near her. These two investigators documented flying objects, bedclothes moving, pools of water appearing on the floor, ghostly apparitions, graffiti on walls, and spontaneous combustion. They witnessed a gruff male voice coming from each of the girls. Janet called herself "Bill" and described himself as an older man. These voices were recorded by BBC but upon later inspection the recording equipment was internally damaged.

Ed Warren, an American paranormal investigator, claimed to have seen Janet levitating while sleeping. He testified that the girls were the subject of demonic possession. Some believed that the girls were the puppets of a demon.

A photo of Janet in midair was disclaimed as a photo of her jumping on a bed. The adult Janet admitted years later that 2% of the claims had been faked. Joe Nickel, an unbelieving reporter, said that the number of hoaxes were closer to 100%. Nickel observed that the poltergeist acted only when no one was present.

These activities were supposedly happening in the years between 1977 and 1979 in a house in Brimsdown, Enfield, England. Professors of psychology Anita Gregory and John Beloff were never convinced of the authenticity of the girl's stories and concluded the girl's imagination was the only reality. Janet and Margaret still attest that the manifestations were real.

With so many taking both sides of this argument, the reader is left to his own deliberance.

CHAPTER FIVE THE PARANORMAL INVESTIGATOR

Paranormal investigators are people that look into the presence of supernatural beings such as ghosts, spirits and demons. Some people are skeptical about the work that these investigators do, because there is no scientific evidence that any of these beings actually exist. However, many people have found comfort from the reassurances that these investigators have been able to provide.

There are two main types of investigators, those that work in the field and those who do not. Some paranormal investigators will visit the property in question to carry out their investigative work. They will use a variety of equipment to detect whether there is a presence from a spirit or ghost. However, there are times when physical investigations such as these are not possible. This may be because the investigator has been asked to look into a case that is in a location that they are not physically able to get to. In these cases, they might use evidence such as witness statements to investigate the case.

Claims of supernatural activity have been made for thousands of years, and there have been people investigating these claims for the same amount of time. The profession of a paranormal investigator has come into the public eye in recent years due to the popularity of TV shows that follow investigators while they are working. This has led to people considering the possibility that supernatural happenings that can't be explained by science actually do occur on an almost daily basis, all over the world.

CHAPTER SIX PARANORMAL INVESTIGATOR MAURICE GROSSE

Maurice Grosse has made a living as a paranormal investigator. He was born in London in 1919 and lived in this country until he died in 2006. He was one of the most famous Enfield Poltergeists investigators that have ever lived.

Maurice received his education at the Regent Street Polytechnic which is located in London. He served in World War II as part of the royal army. His responsibility was to watch prisoners of war that were from Italy. He survived the war but tragedy in his life was far from over. He went home to his family and tragedy turned him onto the world of paranormal.

In 1976 Maurice experienced a great personal loss. His daughter was killed in a motorbike accident. After her death Maurice became interested in psychics and communicating with those that have passed on. He had a number of psychic experiences which caused him to join the Society for Psychical Research as well as the Ghost Club. Maurice was also a member of the Enfield Poltergeists club and spent hours reviewing evidence of encounters with those that have passed on. He is most well known for his work on the Enfield Poltergeist case. He is featured as a major character in the film The Conjuring 2.

Maurice became famous for his work. He appeared on a number of documentaries and gave details about his work. Even skeptics have found Maurice to be credible. He even dared people if they could convince him that his work was not accurate he would pay them a large sum of money. No one was able to prove that Maurice was tricking them. He was really able to communicate with the dead.

Maurice worked on many different cases and even became chairman of this organization. In addition to poltergeists he investigated precognitions as well as psychic photography. He continued to work in this field until the year 2006 when he died.

CHAPTER SEVEN ED AND LORRAINE WARREN

Anyone with an interest in the world of the paranormal will be well acquainted with the names Ed and Lorraine Warren. This husband and wife team are considered to be among the top experts on the spirit world, demonology in particular, in the United States. They are so well known for their expertise in the field and for successfully dealing with spiritual forces that for the past half-century they have been called upon by religious authorities to identify and vanquish spiritual phenomenon of a dark nature when priests or other church officials have come under attack.

Edward "Ed" Warren Miney and Lorraine Rita Moran met as teenagers in their hometown of Milford, Connecticut, where he worked as an usher at the local movie theater Lorraine and her friends frequented. Lorraine later revealed that at the moment she met Ed, she had a psychic revelation that this man was to be her future husband.

Lorraine was born on January 31, 1927. Ed was born on September 7, 1926. Ed served in the United States Navy during WWII, then worked as a police officer prior to becoming an author, lecturer, and self-taught Demonologist. Lorraine's natural abilities as a light-trance medium and clairvoyant made it possible for the two to join forces and work together to become wildly successful paranormal investigators following their marriage on May 22, 1945.

During the early years of their marriage Ed attended Perry Art School, where he pursued his talent for drawing and painting. For a time they supported themselves and their newborn daughter by selling his paintings for the impressive sum of $3-$4 each. While selling his paintings and meeting many different people, if Ed got wind of any place that was rumored to be haunted, he would insist on Lorraine going along with him to check the place out. Ed had an interest in such things after growing up in a house in Bridgeport, Connecticut where a great deal of paranormal activity occurred. Lorraine, however, did not believe in ghosts. It was Ed's desire to investigate such places based on his own experiences in his childhood home that convinced her to go along with her husband on his excursions.

After experiencing firsthand the reality of the spirit world and its effects on the living, the Warrens founded The New England Society for Psychic Research. They had a true passion for the subject and a real desire to help people, both earthbound and those in the Spirit Realm.

Possibly the most famous of the many high-profile cases the Warrens worked on was the haunting of the Perron family of Harrisburg, Rhode Island in 1970. This famous haunting was the subject of the book, House of Darkness, House of Light written by Andrea Perron, one of the children who lived in the home and experienced the haunting firsthand. This case became the basis for the 2013 horror film, "The Conjuring".

Roger and Carolyn Perron and their five children moved into the home, known as the Old Arnold Estate, in the winter of 1970. The family immediately became the victims of vicious attacks by dark forces that filled the old farmhouse. Although every member of the family came under attack, Caroline seemed to draw the worst of the abuse. She repeatedly saw a female apparition which ordered her under threat of "death and gloom" to get out of the house. Through searching old records and photographs, the entity was identified as Bathsheba Thayer, a woman who had lived with her husband and three children near the property in the early 1800s. Bathsheba was rumored among locals to be a practitioner of the Dark Arts, a witch, and the fact that all three of her children all died at very young ages fed this belief. It was said she had sacrificed her daughter to Satan.

When the apparition's torment of Carolyn turned inward and she felt herself being possessed by the spirit of this evil woman, the Perron family contacted Ed and Lorraine Warren for help. Upon their arrival Lorraine immediately sensed a dark presence trying to possess Carolyn. She and Ed set about doing everything they could to dispel the evil presence in the home.

Despite the depiction in the film of the Warrens being able to cleanse the house of the dark presence that permeated it, the true story is that their efforts seemed only to aggravate the presence, which resulted in even more aggressive haunting. The Perrons were not financially able to sell the house and move away until 1980. Even so, the haunting continued after the family relocated to Georgia, though the incidents were reported to have become less violent once away from the Old Arnold Estate.

It is said that the Perron investigation and the events that took place throughout had a significantly detrimental impact on Lorraine Warren, both physically and emotionally. In 2006 Ed Warren passed away. Lorraine served as a consultant on the film 'The Conjuring', based on the Perron family haunting. Today she no longer takes part in paranormal investigations, but she continues to oversee the Occult Museum, a private museum located in Monroe, Connecticut, along with her son-in-law and the Director of the New England Society for Paranormal Research, Tony Spera. She continues to give interviews on a limited basis.

CHAPTER EIGHT THE ENFIELD POLTERGEIST

The Enfield Poltergeist was a case of supernatural events being recorded and observed at a family home in the London suburb of Enfield. The family that lived at the house in question found it really difficult to live there, and their experiences convinced them that something dangerous as well as supernatural was taking place. It was a single parent family and times were not the easiest.

Unsure of what to do next the family asked for help and were sent Ed and Lorraine Warren to investigate what was happening to so adversely affect them. The Warrens were already known in the local area for investigating ghosts, claims of haunting, and spiritual events. What Ed and Lorraine Warren discovered provided evidence of events beyond the physical realm taking place.

The events that would later become infamous began during August of 1977. Divorcee Peggy Hudson lived in a council house in Enfield with her four children after the end of her marriage. Two of her daughters, who were then aged 11 and 13 respectively believed that the house was haunted, or had a demon or poltergeist infesting it. The Police were called out to the address after the first incident. The officer that went to the house saw some furniture move by itself yet could not explain why or how it was able to move without somebody moving it.

Once the tale of unexplained moving furniture spread the house became of interest to the media as well as people interested in finding out about the unexplained. The case attracted so much attention and people interested in paranormal and ghost activity were keen to visit the family and investigate what was going on within its walls. Those people that did visit the Hudson home would come up with various explanations as to the real course of events and if the causes were supernatural or could be scientifically explained. However they tended to want use any evidence to back their ideas about the events been genuinely paranormal, possibly even demonic in nature, or that things had been faked by the two girls with or without the knowledge of other family members. Those approaches meant that the evidence was not collected and used as well as it should have been.

However it was Ed and Lorraine Warren who convinced Peggy Hudson that not only could they explain what was happening in terms of what was wrong in the house, they could also find a solution to set the minds of the children at ease. The Warrens began the investigation with open minds, they did not have any preconceived ideas about events that had taken place and intended to gather as much as evidence as possible to support their eventual findings. The couple already had years of experience is leading such investigations, and would need all of it to deal with events they recorded and witnessed in Enfield.

The Warrens set out to record as much of the activities as they possibly could to gain enough evidence regarding any potential haunting, ghost, or demon presence at the home. They set up cameras and tape recorders to capture as much as possible, and to pick up things they may have been unable to hear or see themselves. Recording things also allowed them to play back film and tapes to check things in greater depth.

BOOK TWO
THE PARANORMAL INVESTIGATORS 2
AMITYVILLE AN ED AND LORRAINE WARREN FILE

CHAPTER ONE 112 OCEAN AVENUE

If I had named this book 122 Ocean avenue how many of you would be reading it? You see that 112 Ocean avenue is the address of the Amityville house made famous in books and countless films.

Thanks to the recent hit horror film the Conjuring 2 there is new interest in the story of Amityville and what happened in that house.

Were the original murders supernaturally inspired?

Was the Lutz family tormented by a demonic force that made them flee their new home only 28 days after moving in?

What did the paranormal investigators Ed and Lorraine Warren believe happened in that house?

The job of a paranormal investigator is mostly to say no nothing is going on here. That there is a logical and natural reason for what has happened. Despite all of the famous investigations that we have heard and read about for every place like the house in Amityville there are dozens that were dismissed as not having any supernatural activity within their walls. This particular story is unique and the dark forces encountered at 112 Ocean avenue is rare.

If you are ready we will begin with the brutal crime that introduced us to this house.

CHAPTER TWO RONALD JOSEPH DEFEO JR.

On Nov. 13, 1974, Ronald Joseph "Butch" DeFeo Jr., 23, committed a grisly crime that captured national attention. The quiet suburb community of Amityville, in Long Island, NY, was rocked by DeFeo's murder of his entire family with a .35 caliber rifle. The case attracted considerable media activity and even spawned the creation of a book and several movies. "The Amityville Horror," authored by Jay Anson and released in 1977, raised the possibility of paranormal entities inhabiting the house where the murders took place.

About the Crime

DeFeo stumbled into a local bar on the night of the incident, claiming that he believed someone had shot his parents, Ronald DeFeo Sr. and Louise DeFeo. He led several people back to his house at 112 Ocean Avenue, where they discovered that indeed his parents had been shot. Also dead were DeFeo's four siblings: Dawn, 18, Allison, 13, Marc, 12, and John Matthew, 9. The police were summoned, and they found all the victims lying face-down on their beds. The parents had been shot two times apiece while the kids were each shot a single time.

Ronald DeFeo initially claimed that a mafia hit man had carried out the executions, but detectives didn't buy it. They were troubled by glaring inconsistencies in his story and kept the pressure on DeFeo. He broke down the next day and confessed to the killings.

Trial and Sentencing

The case went to trial about a year after the murders. DeFeo plead insanity and claimed that he destroyed his family members because they were conspiring against him. Psychiatrists were called in by both the defense and the prosecution. The defendant was found guilty of six counts of second-degree murder, and he was given a sentence of six concurrent terms of 25 years to life.

Oddities About the Killings

It seems unlikely that all six victims would have remained in their bedrooms, lying on their beds, while the perpetrator moved around the house, firing his gun, but that's just what seemed to have happened. Strangely, the neighbors claimed to have heard nothing. No solid motive has been established for the crime although some have speculated that DeFeo did it to collect life insurance money.

Perhaps sensing that everything didn't really add up to a convincing narrative, Ronald DeFeo has made various claims over the years in an attempt to exonerate himself. He stated at various times that one of his sisters committed the homicides, that his sister and an unknown man did it and that he was guilty of the crimes but had help from friends. The authorities have paid him little heed because they consider his tales to be no more than fabrications as evidenced by their outlandishness and the frequency with which they changed.

The Amityville Horror Book

Shortly after Butch DeFeo's conviction, the Lutz family moved into the vacant house at 112 Ocean Avenue, which they purchased through a real estate agent. George Lutz, Kathy Lutz and their three children lasted less than a month in their new living quarters. They fled in terror, claiming that the house was possessed by malign forces.

"The Amityville Horror" by Jay Anson purports to be a true account of what the Lutz family witnessed during their residence in the house where the murders took place. Some of the weird items chronicled by Anson were:

•Strange voices coming from seemingly invisible persons•A hidden room within the building that wasn't on blueprints•Unusual odors with no natural causes•Unexplained damage to windows, doors and locks•Slime seeping out from the walls•Appearance and disappearance of bizarre auditory and visual stimuli

1. The Lutz family allegedly tried to get a Catholic priest to bless the house, but the ritual was interrupted or unsuccessful on multiple occasions. The priest began to suffer from stigmata and health problems. After 28 days, the family called it quits and moved out of the house. The details of their last night at the place were not told because they were supposedly "too frightening."

Public Response

Many criticized the book as being fanciful, unbelievable and clearly fictional. Nevertheless, it served as inspiration for more than a dozen films over the years. Paranormal investigators have looked at the house at 112 Ocean and have reached differing conclusions. Whatever the truth of the matter is, the horrible crime and the location where it took place have captured the public imagination. To this day, many people flock to visit the house whether out of a sense of morbid curiosity or a desire to witness fantastic, supernatural occurrences with their own eyes.

CHAPTER THREE HAUNTED AND EVIL HAUNTINGS

Why are some places considered evil? What do we know about places where things worse than ghosts haunt them, and people are murdered because of this? Is this really what's happening — demonic forces haunt a place and trespassers become susceptible to evil influence? Or are people experiencing echos from the past? A past where something so horrific happened that the emotions felt at the time created a tidal wave of energy that can be felt by others for decades afterward?

There's a credible theory that when something happens to people that makes them feel powerful emotions, an energetic "fingerprint" is left behind. It's said that this "fingerprint" is something that can be felt or experienced by others either in the form of ghosts, or in the form of paranormal activity such as doors closing themselves or frightening sounds coming out of nowhere. If this is true, it could explain millennial of ghost stories and tales of demonic possession.

Others believe that hauntings are the product of imagination. Groups of people will pass down legends from one generation to the next, the stories and myths evolving over years, becoming more believable to the listeners each time. Some say this is where superstition is born. Belief lends a tremendous amount of perceived reliability to the highly imaginative tales told by terrified people who set foot on forbidden ground. However this doesn't explain stories repeated by groups of people who all witnessed the same terrifying hauntings, or multiple individuals who experience paranormal phenomena in a place that nobody expected to be haunted. Perhaps the reason that phenomena like this have never been fully explained is that the hauntings are very real.

If you're open to the idea that paranormal phenomena can occur, it becomes a chicken and egg situation. Some places are considered evil. But which came first, the evil place or the evil people? Take the Amityville Horror for instance. When the Lutz family moved into the house 13 months after DeFeo ruthlessly murdered his family, they moved out abruptly. They said they'd been horribly terrorized by paranormal phenomena. A priest's hands were blistered. Voices ordered them to get out. Father Ralph J. Pecoraro was witness to all of this, and confirmed it himself in an interview. When one asks oneself if the Lutz family moved out because they were too disturbed about the knowledge of what had happened in that house's past and simply let their imagination run away with them, it's difficult to reconcile that with the fact that the priest probably didn't lie. But why did these terrible things occur? Was DeFeo possessed by a demon already present in the house? It begins to seem plausible when one reads the testimonials.

Was the house haunted? By who or what? Previous residents? Demons? Was there a "fingerprint" left behind by the rage of the killer and the blinding terror of the victims? Or was this something more terrifying than the human capacity to terrorize and kill: the presence of powerful demonic forces with the ability to control the actions of human beings? We may never know for sure.

CHAPTER FOUR THE LUTZ FAMILY'S 28 DAYS

On the night of November 13, 1974, a horrific tragedy struck the occupants of 112 Ocean Avenue in Amityville, New York. Twenty-three year old Ronald "Butch" DeFeo Jr shot and killed six family members; both his parents, two brothers and two sisters. All family members were murdered in their bedrooms of the home they occupied at 112 Ocean Avenue.

On July 4, 1975, George and Kathy Lutz were married. On December 18, 1975, the happy newlyweds moved into the home at 112 Ocean Avenue along with Kathy's three children, Daniel, Christopher, and Missy. Due to the tragic events that had occurred thirteen months prior, a priest, Father Ralph Pecoraro, came to bless the house. While blessing the sewing room, Father Pecoraro experienced an unsettling and unexplained coldness on a lovely winter's day. As he sprinkled holy water, an evil, deep voice behind him told him to, "Get out!" The blessing of the house was terminated then. This began a series of unexplained, evil, possibly demonic events that occurred during the short period of time the Lutz' resided at 112 Ocean Avenue. A short time later, unexplained blisters appeared on the priest's hands.

During the short period of time the Lutz' called 112 Ocean Avenue, Amityville, NY home, many strange, peculiar, and truly scary events occurred that led them to believe the house was haunted at best, occupied by a demon at worst. On January 11, 1975, a mere twenty-eight days after moving in, the entire Lutz family fled the house and never returned. They left behind all of their belongings.

While living at 112 Ocean Avenue, youngest daughter, five year old Missy, developed an imaginary friend named Jodie. Jodie was a demonic creature that looked like a pig and had red, glowing eyes. On one occasion, December 25, 1975, George Lutz looked up at the Missy's window and saw a pig standing behind Missy. By the time he got up to her room, Missy was fast asleep, but her small rocking chair was still rocking back and forth. Another night, Missy said Jodie climbed out of her window. Kathy closed the window and saw red eyes glowing at her through the window. This evil entity presented itself to Missy in several other forms, changing at will. Among the forms chose, Jodie would often present herself to Missy as an angel. Was the house simply haunted or was there a demon residing in their home?

The Lutz family was haunted by eerie ominous sounds throughout their home. Bumps and thumps were heard all through the house; with no apparent cause. Locked doors and windows would open and close, but not by a human hand. Hundreds of flies would suddenly swarm the home from out of nowhere. Sickly odors would come out from nowhere. Kathy Lutz was beaten during her sleep by an unseen force, awaking with welts. One frightful night she was levitated off her bed. When the priest that attempted to bless the house tried to contact the family to warn them of the evil lurking in their home, sudden static sounds prevented him from getting the message through.

The Lutz family only lived at 112 Ocean Avenue in Amityville for twenty-eight days. During that short time period, the entire family experienced many horrific, unexplained incidences. We may never know who or what was in that house, but one thing is certain. The Lutz' house was haunted, possibly by an evil demon.

CHAPTER FIVE ED AND LORRAINE WARREN IN AMITYVILLE

In the early morning hours of November 13, 1974, a heinous event took place in a seemingly normal house at 112 Ocean Avenue in the upscale neighborhood of Amityville, New York. Twenty-three year old Ronald "Butch" DeFeo Jr., the oldest of the five children of Louise and Ronald DeFeo, murdered his entire family as they slept peacefully in their beds. Armed with a .35 caliber Marlin rifle, DeFeo first shot his parents to death before moving through the house to also shoot his two brothers and two sisters at point-blank range. All six murders took place in less than 15 minutes and somehow no one else in the neighborhood heard the gunshots and no one else in the home was woken up by the shots that were systematically killing their other family members. After murdering his family DeFeo showered, dressed, gathered his blood-stained clothing and the murder weapon and placed them into a pillowcase, then dumped the evidence in a storm drain as he drove to work at the car dealership owned by his grandfather where both he and his father were employed.

Throughout the work day DeFeo made a show of calling home and receiving no answer, commenting on it to his co workers and wondering aloud why his father hadn't shown up for work that day. Upon returning home that evening, DeFeo pretended to have found his family murdered, running into a local bar screaming for help, claiming a break-in had occurred and someone had killed his whole family.

It didn't take investigators long to figure out what had really happened, especially after finding boxes of ammunition in DeFeo's bedroom that matched the murder weapon. The murders and subsequent arrest of the oldest son galvanized the community. The stories that followed soon gained international attention.

Though there was evidence of conflict between Ronald DeFeo Jr. and his father as well as admitted drug use by DeFeo Jr., he claimed to have been driven to kill his family by "demonic forces" that occupied the home at 112 Ocean Avenue. He said that these evil entities told him to kill them all. Ultimately, Ronald DeFeo Jr. was convicted of six counts of murder and sentenced to six consecutive life terms in prison.

Approximately 13 months later, George and Kathy Lutz and their three children moved into the home. They were aware of it's horrible recent history, but Kathy Lutz later said that this was not an issue for them, saying that "the

DeFeo slayings weren't something that would bother us." The Lutzes were just happy to find a spacious house in such a good neighborhood for only $80,000. Little did they know that only 28 days later they would flee the house in terror, grabbing only a few of their belongings and heading for the safety of Kathy's mother's house close by.

Following their middle-of-the-night departure from their home, George and Kathy contacted Ed and Lorraine Warren with the help of a local television reporter who knew of their work in the field of the paranormal. Ed and Lorraine were a husband and wife team of paranormal investigators. Ed was a Demonologist and Lorraine was Clairvoyant. Both were devout Catholics. On February 24, 1976 the Warrens paid a visit to the home on 112 Ocean Avenue to investigate the claims of paranormal activity.

Immediately upon entering the house Ed Warren felt an "inhuman presence" so powerful that he said he felt as if he was "standing under a waterfall". He said it felt as if the presence was driving him down to the floor. He called upon the name of Jesus Christ and commanded the entity to reveal itself. He said that he knew then that it was no ghost they were dealing with, and no ordinary haunted house.

Lorraine Warren also sensed a demonic presence. She described her impressions of what she encountered in the house: "Whatever is here is, in my estimation,most definitely of a negative nature. It has nothing to do with anyone who has once walked the earth in human form. It is right from the bowels of the earth." It was the Warren's' opinion that the house could only be rid of it's evil entities by a "cleansing", a ritual performed by a Roman Catholic priest or an Anglican exorcist. George and Kathy Lutz had already had one negative experience with having a priest attempt to bless the house the day they moved in. They had asked a local priest, Father Ray Percoraro, to bless their new home. As he went from room to room during the blessing ritual, Father Percoraro was slapped. He also heard a disembodied voice say, "GET OUT!" Following his visit to the house he fell ill with flu-like symptoms,and his hands also began to inexplicably bleed. Based on this past experience, the Lutzes informed Ed and Lorraine that they would not be moving back into the house even if a cleansing ceremony was performed.

Although in the years to come there would be a great deal of speculation as to the validity of the Lutz's claims about the events that took place in the home, the Warrens never wavered in their convictions that the Amityville house was one of the most evil they ever investigated. They were even convinced that an evil entity from the house in Amityville had followed them home.

Ed Warren passed away in 2006. Lorraine Warren has stated adamantly that she would never so much as consider entering the Amityville house again. The Warrens believed that it is entirely possible that Ronald DeFeo Jr. was under the control of the dark forces that dwell in the house at 112 Ocean Avenue in Amityville, New York when he killed his entire family. Throughout their careers as paranormal investigators the Warrens saw many terrible things happen that were either directly or indirectly attributed to demonic forces working through humans. Ed and Lorraine were both experts at recognizing such things and were extremely successful at driving them out in most cases. However, they were unable to deal with the evil that existed in Amityville, the evil that they fully believe cost the entire DeFeo family their lives, by murder and imprisonment for life.

BOOK THREE
PARANORMAL INVESTIGATORS 3
THE EXORCIST, FATHER GABRIELE AMORTH

CHAPTER ONE THE REALITY OF DEMONIC POSSESSION

I have never read horror, nor do I consider The Exorcist to be such, but rather as a suspenseful supernatural detective story, or paranormal police procedural. William Peter Blatty

Accounts of demonic possession predate recorded history. Tales of people being taken over and controlled by demonic forces have been told since the dawn of mankind. The Christian Bible even recounts stories of demonic possession (Matthew 12; Matthew 4; Mark 5). But is it truly possible to be possessed by a demon? Where does this belief come from? Is there any actual proof that possession is real? if so, how does one get rid of the demon?

Although most people in this day and age consider it to be a fictional concept invented by institutions of religion to frighten people into submission or by Hollywood to entertain moviegoers, demonic possession is treated as a very serious matter by the Church. In 1614 the Vatican issues a list of specific guidelines for performing exorcisms. This same set of guidelines was still in existence and was actually updated in 1999. Clearly the Church takes the subject of possession seriously. The Vatican even has a handful of fully-trained Exorcists on staff who are sent out to perform the rites of exorcism whenever a case of possession is brought to the attention of the Church which meets it's criteria: an aversion or physical reaction to holy water, superhuman strength, speaking in unlearned or altogether unknown languages, and more.

A true demonic possession does not take place in a matter of hours or days as is generally portrayed in movies. Possession happens in stages: Manifestation, during which the contact between the demon and human is initially made. This stage of possession is non-invasive and leaves only a slight psychological impression on the individual; Infestation, which occurs when the entity begins to affect the individual in "outside" of his life in ways which call attention to its presence.

The next stage, Mounting, occurs when the individual begins to undergo mental and sometimes physical changes in order for the demon to accommodate itself. In a situation where the person is becoming possessed willfully, he will be able to "feel" the spirit entering his body at this stage. Riding is the next stage, when full possession occurs. The individual does not struggle against it.

The final stage is called Perfect Possession. This is actually a rare state to achieve. It occurs only after repeated possessions and involves the dark spirit and the person being possessed coexisting within the body, working together in all things.

An exorcism is only as effective as the individual's desire to be free of the demon. If the possession has progressed too far, it can be more difficult to exorcise the demon as the individual has become weak and dependent on the spirit. However, rites of exorcism performed by a truly devout and experienced Exorcist have proven to be the most effective way to rid one of an unwanted possession by an evil spirit.

The world may change from one era to the next, but spiritual warfare is as old as Creation itself and ultimately the power of spiritual good triumphs over the darkness of evil almost every time.

CHAPTER TWO THE HISTORY OF EXORCISM

"People shouldn't call for demons unless they really mean what they say."
—C.S Lewis

When most people think of exorcism, the first thing that comes to mind is a certain movie and a little girl with a head that spins backwards who does nasty things with pea soup and even nastier things with a crucifix. This is the Hollywood adaptation of a real-life case of possession and subsequent exorcism which took place in Maryland in 1949.

Robbie Mannheim was a happy, normal 13-year old boy who lived in Cottage City. Maryland. In 1948 Robbie's aunt taught him how to use a Ouija Board. A few weeks later the aunt died. Soon after her death, Robbie's family began experiencing paranormal occurrences in their home. Unexplained noises emanated from empty rooms, objects moved around on their own, scratching sounds could be heard throughout the house, etc.

The family thought that this activity was possibly the recently-deceased aunt attempting to make contact with them from beyond the grave; but when the incidents grew more intense and violent in nature, they realized something sinister was going on. When Robbie became the focal point of the diabolical activity and began acting and speaking differently, the local priest was called upon for help.

Almost immediately it was determined that Robbie was the victim of demonic possession. The priest and other Church authorities approved and sent by the Vatican spent six weeks performing the rites of exorcism over the boy.

They were finally successful in driving out the evil entity, which claimed to be Satan himself, but at great cost to their personal health and well-being. Today Robbie Mannheim works for NASA and claims to have no recollection of any of these events.

Robbie's case is only one of thousands of examples of exorcisms performed in order to rid a human being of an invading evil spirit. Throughout history, exorcisms have been performed in nearly every culture all over the world, in a number of ways and for a number of reasons believed to be related to the presence of malevolent spirits.

In ancient Mesopotamia people believed all illnesses, mental and physical, were caused by evil spirits. Prayers and incantations were offered up to the gods against these spirits to drive them out and heal the afflicted person. In Persia around 600 BC, ancient records show evidence that rituals, prayers, and holy water were used by Zoroaster to conduct exorcisms. Zoroaster was a religious leader who is also considered to have been the first magician. He is credited with being the founder of Zoroastrianism, an ancient religion still practiced today.

The Christian Bible tells of Jesus Christ himself performing exorcisms, calling out and casting away demons who had possessed human beings. Jesus told his followers that they, too, had the power to cast out demons in the name of God. Christianity, like every other religion, has its tenets and instructions dealing with demonic possession and how to perform exorcisms when it has been determined by the church that a true demonic possession exists. In modern times most religious institutions don't like to publicly discuss the subject, but with the current increase in cases of demonic possession and possession by evil spirits, exorcism has become a topic that is being brought more and more often into the light.

If exorcisms have been taking place in one form or another since the beginning of civilization, then there must be something to the practice. Centuries of these rituals, which are still being performed today, can't be wrong.

CHAPTER THREE EXORCISM IN THE MAJOR RELIGIONS

-Yet I think the demon's target is not the possessed; it is us . . . the observers . . . every person in this house. And I think—-I think the point is to make us despair; to reject our own humanity, Damien: to see ourselves as ultimately bestial; as ultimately vile and putrescent; without dignity; ugly; unworthy. -William Peter Blatty

THE RITES OF EXORCISM AMONGST THE WORLD'S RELIGIONS

Exorcisms are a part of the entire world's religion which deals with the world of evil and demons. It's defined as the act of warding off or casting out demons or evil spirits from a person, place, or an object believed to be possessed. Various religions of the world perform the rites of exorcism in different ways and procedures.

Exorcism in Christianity Religion

The revised directions of performing an exorcism consist of a particular section from the Roman Ritual, a book that describes the official rites of the Roman Catholic Church.

To conduct the ritual;

- The priest or exorcist dresses in a purple stole and surplice.

-The rites mostly comprise of a series of prayers, appeals, and statements.

-The exorcist may take some actions at particular times during the ritual such as:

- Sprinkling holy water to everyone surrounding the subject
- Laying hands on the subject
- Making the sign of the cross on both the subject and himself
- Touching the subject with the Catholic relic (usually associated with a saint)

The series of prayers recited during an exorcism are broken down into two:

1) Imploring formula

It's where the priest asks God to free the subject from the evil spirits ("God, whose nature is eternally merciful and forgiving, receive our prayer that your servant, bound by the shackles of sin, may be forgiven by your loving-kindness").

2) Imperative formula

The exorcist demands in the name of God that the evil spirits leave the subject's body ("Depart, wicked one, leave, accursed one, depart with all your deceptions, for God has decreed that man should be his temple").

Though the Roman Catholicism is well known for its rites of exorcism, other Christian denominations also perform the exorcism ritual. Examples are:

- Anglicanism, the Church of England, has every diocese equipped with an exorcist.

-The Lutheran Church bases the exorcism ritual on the biblical declaration that Jesus expelled evil spirits with a single command.

Exorcism in Judaic Religion

The first allusion to exorcism surfaces in the Bible, in the story of David (I Samuel). In the New Testament, Jesus is said to have performed several exorcisms of demonic spirits in the first century. The book of Tobit gives a vivid description of the first exorcism. Josephus recounts events of exorcism in his Antiquities of Jews (2, 5, 8. 45-48).

He describes the procedure of exorcism as:

-the exorcist takes roots of herbs and burns them under the possessed person.

-surrounds the person with water and sometimes it involves immersing the person in the water.

Exorcism in the Islamic Religion

Muslims believe in the concept of a malicious demon. They hold that every individual is assigned a jinni, also called a ham-zaad. The jinni whispers to people's souls so that they submit to evil desires.

Procedure followed during exorcism;

-The possessed person lies down.

-The exorcist puts a hand on the treated person and chants some verses from the Quran.

-Sometimes there is drinking of Holy water.

The exorcist recites particular verses from the Quran. The verses glorify Allah and invoke His help. Sometimes the ah-zan (the call for daily prayers) is also read; this has an impact of expelling the evil or the jinni.

The Islamic exorcism procedure is to recite the last three chapters of Quran (The Fidelity, The Dawn, and Mankind) and seek God's protection from evil.

The Takeaway

Performed to drive out evil spirits from a person, an object, or location; exorcism is universal religion practice. Though each religion has its own ways of performing the ritual, all of them have one single goal of expelling the evil spirits possessing a subject.

CHAPTER FOUR THE CHURCH AS PARANORMAL INVESTIGATOR

When a person is exhibiting odd behaviors people begin to worry. Some of these behaviors may not even seem human. If a person is speaking in a voice that is not their own and speak a language that no one has ever heard before there could be a serious problem. If this person has evil intentions they may be possessed by a demonic spirit. According to the Catholic believes this person may be in need of an exorcism. Before an exorcism takes place there are some things that the Catholic Church may need to do some paranormal investigating before this process begins.

There are some things that the Catholic Church will need to find out before suggesting an exorcism. There are some guidelines that must be followed. A person must be examined by a doctor to make sure they have no physical or mental health issues. In some cases these issues may be treated with modern medicine and this treatment will become more appropriate. This treatment needs to be tried first before an exorcism and shown to be ineffective. Before a full on exorcism some prayer can be used. A paranormal expert from the church will come in and address the situation. They will check out the situation and note if they feel a presence. Some exorcists from the church will be able to feel the demon spirit as soon as they walk into the home or come in contact with the person who is said to be possessed. If there is no reasonable explanation for the behavior it may be time to contact someone from the church to speak about an exorcism.

There are some signs that a demonic presence may have taken over a person. There are some things that a paranormal expert will look for to determine if a person has been possessed. If a person is not eating and has no appetite this may be a sign. This sign will go along with other signs including cutting or biting the skin, a feeling of coldness in the room, and unnatural body postures. If a person goes into a sudden rage and acts out of character it may be the sign of a demonic presence. If a person suddenly starts speaking a strange language especially one that is long forgotten such as Latin than this is a sign that they are not in control of their body. Violent reactions towards religious artifacts can be a sign that a demon is present. If a person has a violent reaction to something such as a cross or the Bible then it is time to call in someone from the church to investigate and help the situation.

If a person is possessed a Catholic Priest will come and help get rid of the demon. They have a special prayer and ritual for an exorcism to rid the body of the demon and bring the person back. It may take more than one exorcism to be successful. While the topic of an exorcism is still taboo to many there are many others within the Catholic religion that feel an exorcism is a real thing and is needed to keep the demons at bay.

CHAPTER FIVE THE EXORCIST GABRIELE AMORTH

- Be sober, be vigilant; because your adversary the devil, as a roaring lion, walketh about, seeking whom he may devour: 1st Peter 5:8

Many believe that exorcism is not real, that demon possession does not actually exist, and that exorcism is basically something that exists in the mind of Hollywood writers and producers. However, there are those who believe it actually does exist in real life, and who actually believe they possess the power to cast evil spirits out of people. One such person is Father Gabriele Amorth, the Roman Catholic Church's leading exorcist.

Who is Gabriele Amorth?

He was born in 1925 in Medina, Emilia. He was ordained a priest of the Catholic faith in 1954. He became an official exorcist in 1986. Over the years Father Medina has performed tens of thousands of exorcisms. By 2000, he reported as many as 50,000 exorcisms. By 2010 this number skyrocketed to at least 70, 000. By 2013, he had hit 160,000.

He is a member of the Society of Saint Paul, according to Wikipedia. This is the congregation founded by James Alberione in 1914.

He has also founded the International Association of Exorcists in 1990, and sat as its president until 2000, and remains honorary president until this day, at age 91, and will be until the day of his death.

Amorth's Advice to Those Wanting to Be Exorcists

It is Amorth's opinion that if you want to be an exorcist, you must be humble, have a life that's based on studying the Word, and on prayer. Also, you must be free of worldly concerns, such as money.

Also you must be a person of great faith. In addition, you must have a good reputation of being a man of prayer, charity, and good judgment.

Books He Has Authored

Father Gabriele Amorth has written two books, specifically on exorcism. The first of these was an Exorcist Tells His Story, and the other was An Exorcism: More Stories. These books were on exorcism as seen through the eyes of Amorth, an exorcist himself.

His Positions on Practices of the Day

Amorth has come out against the whole Harry Potter craze. He is of the opinion that anyone who allows his or her children to watch or take an interest in the series is allowing something that is satanic and harmful for the child. Because of this he has been criticized, especially throughout the non-exorcist clergy, as a bit excessive, one of those people who has allowed his profession to lead him to see Satan everywhere

He has similar views on yoga. He sees it as evil, especially due to its roots in Eastern religion. His critics have criticized him for speaking negatively about other faiths, seeing it as counterproductive.

His Basic Theological Beliefs

According to an excerpt from An Exorcism—More Stories, Amorth believes that Christ is the center of the universe. He believes that everything in it—the sun, the moon, the stars, and its people and animals, were all created for Him. He also believes that that the Christian would be remiss if he didn't at least acknowledge the existence of the kingdom of Satan, from which emanate the very demons he has been attempting to fight throughout his career.

Contrary to his critics that claim that he says that Satan is everywhere, he says, "No he's not. But when he's present, it is painful." He describes the Evil One as a bit of a chameleon who can change form, and speak different languages as well. One of the signs of his presence is the blasphemies coming from the mouth of the person he is possessing. So painfully real is Satan's presence that sometimes it takes a number of Amorth's assistants to hold down someone who is truly possessed of the Devil.

He has been asked by ABC News if the Devil can inhabit the Vatican. He said, "He resides there." He points to the child sex cases emanating from the Vatican as evidence, as well as the murder of his commander by a Swiss guard that took place there.

He is a firm believer in the Virgin Mary. Not just that she was the Mother of Jesus, but that She lives and breathes and still walks with us today and speaks to us too. He speaks of a time when She spoke to a seven year old girl named Jacinta, in Fatima, many years ago, and told her that the chief sin that is going to lead so many souls to Hell is sex sin, which She called "impurity", or the sin of the flesh.

He is, indeed, very theologically conservative when it comes to sexual relationships and the family. He believes, for instance, that divorce and abortion are a disaster. He has cited over 50 million children murdered by abortion. In other words, Amorth firmly believes life begins at conception.

Also, he does not speak well of divorce, euthanasia, or cohabitation, the practice of living together without the benefit of being married. His Views About International Events

It's his view that the emergence of ISIS, the organization known for its mass persecution of Christians, is a sign that we are living in the Last Times, the season that Christ spoke of that would be full of the signs of His imminent return. In recent years ISIS took over an Iraqi Christian town named Qaraqosh, causing the exodus of tens of thousands of people, mainly Christians seeking to get out of persecution's way. ISIS has persecuted and murdered Christians, and people of other non-Muslim faiths in various parts of Syria and Iraq. His view is that this is clearly of Satan.

Putting It All Together

An exorcist for many years, Father Gabriel Amorth says that our biggest mistake is not believing in Satan, who has very dreadful yet real powers. He challenges us, even those who are non-Catholics—to reconsider such beliefs, and to think about Satan in terms of the many who have been delivered by Amorth and those like him. He wants us to consider what it says in the Bible when Jesus delivered people from demons—in terms of how the demons behaved; i.e. the blasphemies against God that would come out of their mouths.

Father Amorth is 90 years old. The time is very close when he will either retire or be taken from this world. However, his body of work will be left for a younger generation to study, like so many that have gone on before him.

References

lifesifenews.com/features/framorth_excerpt1_aug04.asp

abcnews.go.com/travel/chief_exorcist_rev_gabriele_amorth_devil_vatican/story?id=100730110

www.catholicnewsagency.com/news/high-profile-rome-exorcist-isis-is-satan-31600

https://en.wikipedia.org/wiki/Gabriele_Amorth

BOOK FOUR
THE PARANORMAL INVESTIGATORS 4
THE BORLEY RECTORY, A HARRY PRICE FILE

CHAPTER ONE THE SPR

The Society for Psychical Research (SPR) is a parapsychological organization whose purpose is to research and understand occurrences of paranormal activity, reports of psychic individuals, and anything else under the paranormal umbrella. Parapsychology by definition is the scientific study of the ways organisms communicate and interact with one another and their surroundings in ways that are thus far not explainable using typical, existing scientific models. The SPR was founded in 1882, a few months after a fateful conversation between physicist William F. Barrett and journalist Edmund Rogers occurred in 1881. Its first president was Henry Sidgwick, and the organization's membership included numerous renowned individuals such as Arthur Conan Doyle.

The SPR, still active today, is unique among paranormal investigators because of their staunchly scientific approach. Rather than leap to the conclusion that all reports of paranormal activity and psychic phenomena are necessarily evil, always good or utterly and inherently false, they remain neutral and open to the possibility that parapsychological research has great merit. These aren't amateurs; SPR's trustees and officers generally hold multiple degrees, and the membership includes doctors, scientists, PHDs, and ordinary people. Since the membership is diverse, so are the multidisciplinary research methods. The academic background of the Trustees and Officers lends legitimacy and credibility to their work, especially when the SPR releases information about psychic and paranormal activity that would otherwise raise skepticism or even ridicule in the media and scientific community. It's safe to say that the Society for Psychical Research is a highly legitimate organization with a firm foundation whom have been successfully researching and documenting poltergeists, psychics and other paranormal activity for well over a century.

It's worth drawing special attention to Henry Sidgwick. He was noteworthy as a paranormal investigator because he was relentless in his exposure of fake mediums and fortune-tellers. However his practices allowed the people who likely had real capabilities to rise up to a place of higher respectability and furthered the understanding of what real psychic activity looks like. He's remembered by many as an esteemed researcher to this day.

The SPR's research about poltergeists is monumental. Innumerable accounts of poltergeists have been recorded and researched. The most notable — and the ones that helped to establish this activity as substantive — include cases where sounds can be recorded or where letters are written posthumously by the dead. One look up the SPR's recordings of the sounds that poltergeists make, and can see, when a computer generated visual is produced, how different the sounds made by a poltergeist versus the sounds made by the living are.

Also heavily researched by the SPR are unexplained lights and orbs, demonic possession, morphic resonance (transference of thoughts or ideas to other people) and mirror reading (commonly understood as crystal ball gazing). Of particular interest to many people are their reports on angelic beings, life after death experiences, and the appearance of deceased relatives. With their vast library of publications, one can get lost in the SPR's paranormal research archives for an eternity.

CHAPTER TWO THE BORLEY RECTORY A HAUNTED HISTORY

During ancient times, in the thirteenth century, a monk fell in love with a nun. They decided to run away and elope to build and establish a new life for themselves. While in the process if running away, before even embarking on this wonderful journey, their lives were cut short. While the monk was hung to death, the nun endured a worse fate. She was walled up inside the cold, brick monastery walls- while she was still alive.

Built on the site of the ancient monastery where the two lovers met their tragic demise, the Borley Rectory has become known as the most haunted house not only in England but in the entire UK. Despite warnings from locals that the site, commonly referred to as the "Nun's Walk", was haunted, Reverend Henry Bull built his rectory in 1863. Immediately, strange occurrences took place that gradually became stronger and more horrific with each new tenant. This lasted until the fire that took the life of the Borley Rectory in 1938. Many believe the site is still haunted to this day.

In 1863, Reverend Henry Bull built the Borley Rectory and him and his family moved in. Almost immediately, they began seeing an apparition of a nun strolling along, roaming the property. The reverend was not fearful and thought this was entertaining. He built a summerhouse on the property so him and his son, Harry, could sit and watch the nun on her walk while they enjoyed after-dinner cigars. Guests, servants, the reverend himself, his son, and his four daughters all witnessed this phenomenon, as well as others. Other sightings at the time included the nun peering out the rectory windows.

When Reverend Henry Bull passed away, in the Blue Room of the Borley Rectory, his son inherited the home. The hauntings and sightings increased upon Henry's passing. In addition to the nun roaming the grounds, a ghostly horse drawn carriage was now seen racing around. During this period of time, the ghosts were peaceful. The only signs of ghosts were the appearance of the nun and horse drawn carriage, mysterious, unexplained footsteps, and strange creaking sounds.

After Harry Bull passed in 1927, Reverend Guy Smith became the new tenant of the Borley Rectory. The ghastly hauntings were too much for him to handle and he swift fully departed within one year. During the short period of time that the Smith's resided there, they called in famous ghost-hunter Harry Price. While visiting, Harry Price had a vase and stones thrown at him by unseen forces.

As the intensity of the terrifying hauntings, unexplained sightings, and strange occurrences worsened, reverend Lionel Foyster and his wife Marianne became the new tenants of the frightful Borley Rectory. The Foyster's would often become unexplainably locked out of rooms, their personal belongings would vanish without a trace, windows and other items would suddenly smash, and strange noises could be heard throughout the house. Writings asking Marianne for help would suddenly appear out of nowhere on the walls; some even as people stood and watched. The Foysters attempted to have the Borley Rectory exorcised, but to no avail. Marianne was thrown from her bed to the floor by unseen hands, and attacked by an unseen force. The Foysters logged and reported close to 2,000 horrific paranormal incidences to Harry Price before moving out in 1935.

The ghost hunter Harry Price leased the Borley Rectory next, for one year, to perform a deep investigation into these terrifying hauntings. He and his crew of investigators monitored and documented all of the fascinatingly terrifying events and ghastly activities that occurred. A séance was performed in which a spirit threatened the house would burn down that night and the bones of a nun's body would be found in the rubble.

After the one year lease was up, Captain Gregson moved in. His two dogs mysteriously disappeared and he was subjected to the same haunted circumstances as his previous tenants. Eleven months after moving into Borley Rectory, an oil lamp fell over, even mysteriously, or by Captain Gregson himself, and the building was burned to the ground. In 1943, a digging led by Harry Price uncovered the bones of a young woman. Harry Price gave the bone a real Christian burial, but the hauntings and strange occurrences at the eerie site continue to go on today.

CHAPTER THREE MEDIUM STELLA CRANSHAW

Stella Cranshaw, born Dorothy Stella Cranshaw in 1900, was a London born woman from the 20th century who wasn't exactly your average English girl. The daughter of a charcoal burner and a London nurse, Cranshaw boarded a train in 1923 where, by stroke of chance, she met Harry Price. This would be the beginning of her career as a psychic.

Harry Price, born 1881, was a British paranormal and haunting researcher of the early 1900s. He is most famous for his Borley Rectory investigation in which he lived in a purportedly haunted rectory building for a year and wrote his findings in a book he later published, giving the Borley Rectory the title of "most haunted house in England." In 1923 he, along with many of his contemporaries, were fascinated with finding a real medium or psychic. Price was getting tired of all the hoaxes and fakes in his search for a true medium. That's where Stella Cranshaw turned his luck.

While on the train, Cranshaw become bored and noticed Price had a stack of magazines in front of him. She asked to borrow a copy of the paranormal magazine, Light, and they had a long and fateful conversation. Over the course of the train ride, Cranshaw told Price about her several experiences with paranormal incidents. Among the phenomenon she experienced were cool breezes when all the windows were closed, unexplained flashes of light, and small objects floating without cause. Price believed she might be psychic and convinced her to participate in a series of séances to help his research.

Cranshaw ultimately took hand in three series of séances which each consisted of several sessions over the course of 6 years. These all took place in very controlled environments which Price labored over to ensure no fraud could take place. Several of Price's own inventions were used and he also brought in trusted colleagues to help with the sessions. None of Cranshaw's personal affects were allowed in the room, the furniture was set up in such a manner that actions could not be hidden from view, the room was locked and the key taken away, and Cranshaw's hands and feet were under the control of those in the room with her.

The first session took place in March of 1923 at the National Laboratory of Psychical Research. The second occurred on April 10th, 1926. Cranshaw's final séance was performed in 1928, after which she and Harry Price parted ways and she ceased to use her abilities. Cranshaw showed extreme physical and emotional exhaustion after her séances and her powers seemed to become less prominent as time went on. It is also possible that Cranshaw lost interest in or desire to use her abilities.

During the sessions Cranshaw and the others in the room experienced an array of events. There were often flashes of light, strange tapping sounds, and ominous levitation of smaller objects and even furniture. The temperature of the room often fluctuated toward cold during her episodes with cold breezes that at one point dropped the temperature from 63 to 43 degrees. During a singular session furniture being levitated was completely destroyed.

In her most powerful sessions, Cranshaw saw a being she stated was Palma. Many paranormal scholars believe this to be her spirit guide. Her most powerful and cited insight was when she claimed to see a newspaper with the name "Andrew Salt" written in bold letters on it. There was a falling boy on it that doctors kept pouring a white powder over. Over a month later a newspaper ad for Andrew's Liver Salt was printed on the front page featuring a picture of a boy who had knocked some salt off his plate. This was taken by many to be proof of premonition.

Given the great lengths Harry Price went to in order to ensure authenticity, many psychic researchers regard Stella Cranshaw as a true psychic and Price's reports on her to be a great resource. The reports still reside at the Harry Price Library at the University of London.

CHAPTER FOUR INVESTIGATING THE BORLEY RECTORY

Dubbed "Most Haunted Place In England" by journalists, paranormal researchers, and supernatural enthusiasts around the globe, the Borley Rectory is one of the most documented and notorious hot spots for paranormal activity. Although skeptics and critics alike, have had their reasons to dispute the alleged events that have taken place in this rural England locale, nearly 80 years' worth of chilling and unexplained phenomena has made it hard to sweep this story under the rug. The history of this eerie and mysterious place reads like a rap sheet of misfortune, begging the question of where did it all begin? Even before Harry Price, pioneer of the paranormal realm was summoned to take on the case, numerous reports of sightings and rumors of tragedy had been too overwhelming to ignore. The disturbing details uncovered in Harry Price's Borley Rectory Investigation have taken this controversial ghost story to legendary status. Adorned with stark peaks pointed to the sky like daggers, the Gothic style mansion lives up to its harrowing reputation. The timeline of historical events that took place at Borley Rectory set the scene, if not foreshadowed the trail of tragedy this notorious legacy has left behind. According to rumor, the land the rectory was built on was doomed long before its existence. Paranormal activity reports back all the way to the 13th century where a monastery was built prior to the rectory. A rumor that has been passed down generation to generation places blame for the paranormal mayhem on an illicit affair between a monk and a nun leading to their tragic death. The monk was executed, while the nun met a much worse fate; buried alive brick-by-brick. Some have even claimed a poltergeist tied to the land has been wreaking havoc since the Crusades. Since then, each successor has been met with a downward-spiraling slew of misfortune all the way until its demise during a fire in 1939. The deaths of two owners in the Blue Room of the rectory, alleged exorcisms, infidelity, and vanishing pets are just a handful of the copious amount of calamity that have occurred. Apparitions of headless horseman are commonly seen around the property. They are rumored to be the ghosts of the beheaded coachmen who tried to help the nun and her forbidden lover elope. The earliest sightings described have been of a nun roaming the gardens and then vanishing into thin air. The original builder and owner of the Borley Rectory Reverend Bull, built an addition to the house overlooking the gardens where sightings of the nun frequently appeared. Others have heard bells ringing, footsteps, and seen lights in windows when vacant. The large outcry from servants, spectators, and the Smith family who occupied the rectory at one point, lead to the local newspaper requesting Harry Price's expertise to evaluate the phenomena. Price wasn't new to the rectory when he returned for a second time to examine new, wilder claims he later referred to as "16 hours of thrills", made by the Foyster family. Marianne Foyster later admitted to fabricating the events that happened while they lived there to distract from an extra-marital affair she was having. Although her confession added to the disbelief of Price's credibility, the findings from his previous and subsequent journeys with other occupants long outlived the doubts. Upon his first encounter with the rectory, immediate paranormal activity was strongly felt. He was met with various objects violently being thrown around the room and down staircases. Vases, candles, coin and rocks were seen flying throughout the estate. The daughter was thrown from her bed and almost suffocated by her mattress. The place remained vacant a few years before Harry Price took out a year- long lease to conduct an official investigation. During this time he placed an ad to recruit unbiased participants to stay for various amounts of time and record anything and everything they saw. Each were given an Ouija board and encouraged to use it. The events that took place during the investigation, including Price's creation of the ghost-hunting kit, have been both controversial and entrepreneurial for the field of Paranormal Research. One of the most chilling events that took place during this investigation was when a man named Mark Kerr-Pearse was eating alone inside of the rectory and was locked into the room. He first heard the turn of a key, and then much to his dismay realized it was being locked from inside, as he could see the key turning in the bolt by itself. During one of many séances conducted during his investigation, a bar of soap was said to have jumped into the air off the floor. Price mentioned in his writings that after the gardener and him chased after the ghost of the nun, a large pane of glass came crashing to their feet. Other participants have described the sound of a heavy dog panting over them while they slept. Perhaps the most significant of all the paranormal activity to take place, was a series of séances where contact with several spirits was made. The first spirit belonged to a nun who was murdered by her husband and buried within the property; her bones were purportedly excavated by price at a later date. Another spirit predicted that the rectory would fall victim to a fire, which it did less than a year later.

Despite the surmounting opposition to Price's work during the Borley Investigation, rumors of paranormal activity still lurk among the grounds where it once stood to this day. Generations of families who shared this creepy dwelling in common, have each contributed to the legacy that is still hot on the press. Nonetheless, throughout his work Harry Price has indubitably proven himself as a talented author, paranormal investigator, and a clever man.

CHAPTER FIVE HARRY PRICE PARANORMAL INVESTIGATOR

In the world the paranormal and psychics many people do not believe in the ability that a person can communicate with the dead. Other feel that there are selected people with a gift that allows them to be able to communicate with those that have past and see events that did not happen yet. While there are some frauds that give people with this gift a bad name no one can dispute the gift that was given to Harry Price. He was a British psychic researcher as well as author. He gained fame for exploring those fake Spiritualists and was an investigator into the phenomenon of psychics. One of his most famous paranormal investigations was the Borley Rectory in Essex, England that was said to be haunted.

Harry Price was born in 1881 in London. He attended school at the New Cross and later at the Haberdasher's Aske Hatchman Boys School. When he was a teenager he wrote a number of dramatic plays as well as some of the interactions he had with poltergeists as a child. Many of his plays took place in locations that were said to be haunted.

By 1908 Price was studying archaeology and got job working at a paper merchant. He also wrote for two papers in the Sussex area. Price became interested in the paranormal a joined a group called the Magic Circle. This group had an interesting in magic and conjuring. At this also sparked his interested in the investigation of paranormal activity. He worked with another psychic researcher named Eric Ding wall and learned about the fraudulent practices of those claiming to communicate with those that have past.

By 1920 Price has an interest in the paranormal that he could not deny. He became a member of the Society for Psychical Research and was able to point out a number of magicians and those said to be spirit medium that were fraudulently practicing in this area. One of his earliest research projects was in 1922 when he investigated William Hope who claimed to have the ability to photograph spirits. He exposed him as a fraud and was able to find out how he was producing the pictures of so called spirits. This was one of his first successes. Price went on to investigate a number of others. He has to learn all of these tricks. While many of these so called experts were good at their craft they were no match for Price and his investigative techniques.

By 1926 Price became well known in this area and his research he was able to form his own organization called the National Laboratory of Psychical Research. He tested a number of spirit mediums and was able to tell which ones were able to communicate with those that have passed and which ones were making it up. He also found out the techniques on how a medium can fool the average person that is not educated in this field.

Price was offered a position at the University of London where he was part of the Department of Psychical Research. This department had the equipment he needed to conduct further research and educate others in this field. He also joined the Ghost Club and was a member until it closed in the year 1936.

Many experts in this field praised Price for his work. Richard Wiseman was another skeptic and he praised Price for being able to expose fraudulent mediums. Price was not only a skeptic but he was a scientist and had the knowledge and the research to study those that claimed to be blessed with the paranormal gift. Price was said to be one of the most fascinating figures in research and had methods that can be used by other investigators today. Price was said to pave the ways for other investigates including Ed and Lorraine Warren. These modern researchers use some of the techniques used by Price in order to debunk so of the modern mediums that claim to have the ability and the gift of communicating with the afterlife.

There are some famous mediums that Price was able to expose as being fakes. Eileen Garret was said to be able to make contact with the spirit world. Price invited her in to conduct a séance at his research center. She claimed she was able to make contact with the spirit of Herbert Carmichael Irwin. Two days after their meeting the R101 disaster happened. Some say the contact with the spirit world lead to this disaster. According to Price he was skeptical that Garret was really able to make contact with the spirit world. He said she was good at her craft but was a fraud. He also stated that she appeared to be in a trace and was convincing but her alleged contact had no effect and did not lead to this disaster. Some have even said that she had prior knowledge to the layout of the building where this incident happened and was able to repeat the information that she learned.

Price continued his research until the year 1948. He was at his home in Pulborough, West Sussex and suffered from a major heart attack. According to those close to him this heart attack almost instantly killed him. His widow gave some of his research to the University of London. This information including correspondence, drafts of his research that was not yet published, papers with libel cases, some of the reports on his investigations, and photographs. This information would be used to help other studying in this field and show them techniques on how to debunk mediums that are participating in fraudulent practices.

Price was a researcher that was before his time. He did not like people that were in a desperate time in their lives being taken advantage of those that were out to defraud them and take their money. While some people may have the gift to be a true medium there are others that are in the business of exploiting people. Price dedicated his life to conducting research to expose those who were in the business of fraud while establishing himself as one of the greatest paranormal investigators.

BOOK FIVE
THE PARANORMAL INVESTIGATOR 5
GAURAV TIWARI DEATH OF A GHOST HUNTER

CHAPTER ONE. THE INDIAN PARANORMAL SOCIETY

-The boundaries which divide Life from Death are at best shadowy and vague. Who shall say where the one ends, and where the other begins? - Edgar Allan Poe

With a population of over 1 billion people, India is one of the most densely populated countries in the world. This fact, along with it's location and long history of ancient spiritual practices guarantees that it is a land rich in paranormal activity. Even so, no serious, legitimate group dedicated to the study of paranormal activity existed in India until 2009, when Gaurav Tiwari founded the Indian Paranormal Society Tiwari had absolutely no interest nor belief in the paranormal whatsoever until an incident in 2003 changed his mind. He was in a hotel room in Florida when he encountered the apparition of a young girl. It was this event that made him a die-hard believer in the supernatural and led him to form the investigative group. He studied and became a certified paranormal investigator. He established the Indian Paranormal Society in order to educate the people of his country regarding matters of the paranormal and to help them to overcome their archaic, per-conceived notions regarding the spirit world.

The Indian Paranormal Society formed a research team called Ghost Research and Investigators of Paranormal (G.R.I.P.). This team investigated paranormal occurrences throughout India. Gaurav Tiwari was the team's lead investigator. As they conducted more and more investigations, their work became more widely known. Some people, particularly those who had been affected by some type of paranormal activity, believed wholeheartedly in the work that the Society was doing. Others, especially those who were older and who had deeply-rooted spiritual and religious beliefs, dismissed it.

Most of the Indian people considered the Indian Paranormal Society to be some sort of "modern nonsense", new to the country and not to be taken seriously. However, once the group began doing extensive, in-depth investigations and televising them the Society - and the subject of the paranormal in general - began to be taken seriously by the people of India. The public began to ask questions and to share their own personal experiences with the paranormal.

As a result, the Indian Paranormal Society has grown in popularity, expanding their investigations all over the country.

Tragically, on July 7, 2016, Gaurav Tiwari was found unresponsive and mortally wounded in the bathroom of his home in India under very unusual circumstances. a thud was heard in the bathroom followed by the rattling of the door, as if someone was coming out. When Tiwari had not emerged after about an hour someone went to check on him. When he did not respond to three knocks on the door, guests in the home forced their way into the bathroom and discovered Tiwari on the floor, eyes bulging, gasping for breath. He was rushed to the hospital where he died before treatment of any kind could be administered. The only visible marking on Tiwari's body at the time of his death was a deep black mark on his neck. Ghost hunters and paranormal experts alike indicate that this type of mark is a sign of revenge by evil spirits in distress. To this day no exact cause of death for Tiwari has been identified in the matter.

The Indian Paranormal Society continues to operate and investigate supernatural incidents throughout India.

CHAPTER TWO THE DANGERS OF GHOST HUNTING

-We cannot banish dangers, but we can banish fears. We must not demean life by standing in awe of death. - David Sarnoff

On July 7, 2016, Gaurav Tiwari, founder and lead investigator of the Indian Paranormal Society died under very unusual circumstances. Guests in his home heard a thud come from a bathroom occupied by Tiwari, followed by the sounds of the door rattling as if someone were trying to open it, but it remained closed. After approximately an hour, a guest went to check on Tiwari. When he did not respond after three knocks on the door, guests broke the door down and discovered Tiwari unconscious on the floor, eyes bulging, gasping for breath. He was rushed to the hospital where he died a short time later. The only visible marking on his body at the time of his death was a deep black mark on his neck. Ghost hunters and paranormal experts alike agree that this type of mark denotes an act of revenge by evil spirits in distress. To date, no cause of death has been identified for Tiwari.

Those who are involved in investigating paranormal matters open themselves up to a number of dangers, spiritual, physical, and otherwise. In particular, those who are involved in ridding dwellings or people of unwanted spiritual activity or attachment are susceptible to often violent attacks from entities who are angry at their interference. Physical attacks are common. Investigators are often scratched, burned, bitten, hit, choked, etc, and in some cases the harm is much more severe, resulting in hospitalization or, in the most extreme cases, death.

Attacks can also come in the form of possession, with the spirit choosing to turn its attentions on the investigator rather than the victim the investigator is attempting to help. When this happens, the investigator's entire family can be affected, as the entity can invade their home and become violent while working to possess it's new victim.

It is also common for spirits to attack the mental or physical health of the paranormal investigator. Many an investigator has been forced to give up their profession after becoming mentally or physically incapacitated due to spiritual attack.

For those who are skeptical about the world of the supernatural, these claims may seem less than valid. However, for those whose lives have been di-

rodney cannon

rectly affected by entities from the Other Side, the dangers of being a ghost hunter are terrifyingly real.

CHAPTER THREE PARANORMAL BELIEFS IN INDIA

Introduction

There is a strong paranormal tradition in India. Almost all countries and cultures have their own ghost stories and their own convictions that there are evil spirits and malevolent supernatural beings. Supernatural beings and evil spirits are partly manifestations of insecurities that tend to be nearly universal to the human experience. However, these beliefs are more common and popular in some cultures. The modern world has made something of an uneasy and incomplete transition to rationalism. While many rationalists in India protest the persisting beliefs in the supernatural, paranormal beliefs still persist in many Indian cultures to this day.

Bhoot Ghosts

One interesting thing about a lot of superstitions and legends is that they tend to vary from city to city and not just from country to country. Talking about Indian superstitions is somewhat misleading, since some of them are really only popular in certain parts of the country. There are certainly Indian superstitions that are more popular across the country of course. However, many individual cities in India have their own ghosts. The belief in ghosts is particularly strong in India because according to Hindu tradition, it is not possible to destroy the soul. As such, the soul can return in many different ways.

The bhoot is a type of male ghost that a lot of people believe to be real in India. It uses black energy in order to taunt and haunt its descendants. There have actually been Bollywood films featuring the bhoot, which demonstrates the widespread popularity of this creature, even if not all Indians actually believe in it personally.

Bhoots are shape shifting ghosts. While they often appear in a human form, plenty of them also manifest as animals. They have backwards-facing feet, which is one of the ways that people can distinguish them as ghosts. They often appear in white clothing and specifically haunt the areas where they were killed. Bhoot spirits more or less bathe in milk, and it's believed that drinking milk that has been contaminated by bhoot spirits can lead to a demonic possession. Bhoot spirits supposedly also talk in a sort of nasal voice that manages to give them away, and this is one of the signs that people are supposed to look for when trying to identify a bhoot.

People can supposedly ward off bhoot ghosts using water or objects made from iron. Warding off evil spirits with water is fairly commonplace in superstitions. Burning turmeric is also supposed to get rid of them.

Other Ghosts

Pretas are other male ghosts, and they're specifically the ghosts of Hindu men who experienced violent deaths. Pretas are also created when their families don't observe the proper burial rituals. Essentially, they act as cautionary tales for families who want to forgo proper burial protocol.

The Hadal is a type of female goblin, demonstrating that there are ghosts and evil spirits of all genders in this canon. They specifically dig out buried bodies in cemeteries to use in their evil rituals. In that regard, they seem similar to necromancers and black magic practitioners.

There is also a female version of a bhoot called Achudail. This is a spirit that forms after a woman dies in pregnancy or in labor. Many of the features of achudail are similar to those of normal people, but they have been inverted in some way or another. Like bhoots, they have backwards-facing feet. Young men supposedly find chudail spirits at fields or road crossings. Generally speaking, loving achudail is supposedly fatal to the young man who loves her. However, some stories maintain that it is possible for a human man and achudail to marry.

Haunted and Portentous Trees

Given the rich plant life of India, it shouldn't surprise anyone to know that specific tree species are believed to be the favored habitats of certain malevolent beings. Many people believe that ghosts hide out in Peepul trees, and that it's a good idea to steer clear of them when it gets dark outside. Many people stay away from Banyan trees for the same reason.

Some people more or less believe that Sal trees can be used to detect the presence of witches. If a person writes the name of an alleged witch on the branch of a Sal tree, that branch will die. This belief is particularly strong in Jharkhand.

Possession

Many people in India actually report spiritual possessions. Exorcists have no trouble finding work when it comes to expelling evil spirits in India. Many of the evil spirits that they specifically try to get rid of are bhoot spirits, since it is often maintained that consuming bhoot contaminated milk can lead to a possession. The consumption of milk and dairy products is common in India, so it would follow that bhoot possessions would also be common.

Nocturnal Superstitions

The belief that bad things happen at night is found in almost all cultures. However, nighttime superstitions vary from culture to culture. In India, it's believed that sweeping the floor at night can cause bad luck. If nothing else, it's a good excuse to avoid doing chores.

Naturally, people are usually going to have to be particularly wary of almost all ghosts and other spirits at night. It seems that there are few that specifically prey on people during the day. People avoid all haunted sites at night, even though they typically avoid them during the day as well.

Conclusion

People might find that the belief in spirits in India is not all that different from what they might find in other places. There are certain elements in folklore that manage to appear over and over again. Paranormal and spiritual beings address humanity's fear of the dark, fear of death, and general fear of the unknown. However, the different ways in which those fears and concerns manifest can be interesting. The rationalists of the world and the rationalists of India might try to ward off these spirits in a different way, but even they might find the individual stories fascinating.

CHAPTER FOUR. THE LIFE AND DEATH OF GAURAV TIWARI

If you've followed the world of paranormal investigations, you'll know that the best ghost hunters are not plumbers or guys in tight tee shirts with spiky well-styled hair. The United States did seem to have cornered the market for ghost hunting shows until the arrival of Indian pilot turned metaphysical and scientific paranormal explorer Gaurav Tiwari.

Gaurav Tiwari was born on September 2, 1984, His family was Hindu and did not believe in spirits or ghostly phenomenon. The son of a successful family, he did some acting work at age 16 before going to the United States to train as a commercial pilot in 2007. As part of his training package, he was lodged in an apartment in Florida. This was a move that would challenge his former ideas as a skeptic. Soon things began happening that changed his mind about activity directed by those in the afterlife. Most notably, he witnessed stunning poltergeist activity in his apartment.

This spirit encounter led him on a path of paranormal exploration. He began studying the world of the metaphysical and earn certifications as a UFO Investigator and Lead Paranormal Investigator. Gaurav Tiwari earned the title of Reverend when he was ordained by the International Church of Metaphysical Humanism, http://www.metaphysicalhumanism.org/,

He came back to India trained as a pilot as well as a paranormal investigator, and looking for phenomena won out over pursuing a conventional career as a commercial pilot. Gaurav Tiwari founded the Indian Paranormal Society in 2009, which was the first ghost hunting society in India to use the scientific approach to distinguish spirit activity from naturally explainable phenomena. He also used his gifts to train as a hypnotist, which came in handy during paranormal investigations to help calm and center other participants.

Tiwari boldly went where others were afraid to go, namely the chiller slab in a morgue. During an investigation, one of his Australian team members got on the tray and then had to jump off due to fear. Tiwari who always wanted to analyze what he fears, or what other fear, he gladly hopped up on the table, and let them shut him in the locker, camera in hand. Although he was still on crutches from an injury, nothing slowed down his quest for knowledge and curiosity of the inexpiable.

Unlike other paranormal ghost hunting shows where the investigators act, or rather overact for the camera to display dramatic effect,Gaurav Tiwari retained his placid, professional demeanor whether he saw a full body apparition or visited the most frightening well-known areas of paranormal activity. He appeared on Haunted Weekends,Bhoot Aaya, and Fear Files, as well as many news programs around the globe, according to the India Times,http://www.indiatimes.com/news/india/the-life-and-death-of-guarav-tiwari-the-ghost-hunter-who-ended-the-supremacy-of-supernatural-sadhus-258227.html.

One of his most challenging assignments was MTV Girls Night Out, where Tiwari and his team had three Indian female celebrities along to investigate a hostel. One of the girls, defined as a believer, got so scared that she couldn't speak, but Tiwari quickly, yet calmly removed her from the scary surroundings. On another investigation in Australia, one of the teammates had an irrational phobia of horses. As they were riding out on horseback to do the investigation, Tiwari refused to just leave him behind. He put his hypnosis skills to work and asked team member Ian to visualize two TV screens, one in black and white with his fears and one color television showing him without this fear. You can check out a clip of this and more of his best investigations on YouTube,https://www.youtube.com/watch?v=LbO8MIz_I7k.

Throughout his career, he participated in over 80 paranormal investigations, most times taking the lead. He awakened an interest in scientific investigation in India and became famous in his country as a metaphysical expert.

He wasn't afraid to debunk myths and hoaxes and used the scientific approach in all of his research. From the strange case of a worker who came back to her office after a holiday but had died 20 days earlier. to cases that he could rule out due to hysteria, hallucinations and other phenomena. He concentrated on verifiable data, such as electromagnetic fields, sound recordings, and temperature changes. He only alluded to something being "paranormal" if the phenomena defied all rational scientific explanation through rigorous testing. One of his most famous, and surprising debunking was the claim that Bhangarh Fort was haunted. His conclusions did not come up with any paranormal entities or energy at the investigation. This contradicts the claims of many who have had experiences visiting the historic fort, as well as mediums and Indian Spirit Doctors who have claimed the site to be haunted.

The strangest part of Gaurav Tiwari's life was his unexpected death on July 7, 2016. His wife said that despite rumors of marital problems between her and Gaurav, he was in good spirits. No one knew anything was wrong until they heard a noise coming from the bathroom. Upon opening the door, they found Gaurav Tiwari on the bathroom floor in his Delhi home with a black mark around his neck. Despite being rushed to the hospital and put on a ventilator to facilitate breathing, Mr. Tiwari could not be revived. Police say it was suicide or possibly homicide by a human; however, there are many who question these determinations. He was only 32 years old and his life revolved around his work and family. Tiwari was also a devoted yoga practitioner and woke every morning at 4:30 am. His family is heartbroken at his unexpected loss as well as fans that say the idea that his death was a suicide just doesn't add up. Gaurav had just signed a contract to begin filming a new paranormal show starting later that July, so why would he commit suicide weeks before the show was to start. When the family called a neighbor to break down the locked door after hearing no noise from the bathroom, Tiwari was alone. His father Uday Tiwari said that he would never have killed himself and had just been married earlier in the year. He told the India Times, http://www.indiatimes.com/news/india/the-life-and-death-of-guarav-tiwari-the-ghost-hunter-who-ended-the-supremacy-of-supernatural-sadhus-258227.html, that he could not commit further on his son's death, as it was still under investigation. Despite the lack of a conclusive theory on his death, various rumors appeared online. It is reported that one of his teammates from Haunting Australia, Allen Tiller, wrote a post on Facebook claiming that the cause was due to a sudden heart attack, which is unfounded in any medical diagnosis or fact.

http://indiatoday.intoday.in/story/gaurav-tiwari-paranormal-investigator-foung-dead-mysteriously/1/712551.html.

Police questioned his wife and other family members due to rumors of marital strife and infidelity, suspecting it was perhaps a homicide. No further clues have come from those hours of questioning. Nothing on his mobile phone or e-mails suggested depression or despair. He posted on social media the day before he died and no reason for self-harm could be found. He was not suffering from any financial difficulties, according to many sources. There is some talk of an argument between him and his new wife because she was upset about his late night ghost hunting, but as that was his occupation, this doesn't seem like a serious problem that would lead to suicide or murder.

There are other possible reasons for his sudden demise, believers say. One odd clue was that from the inside of the bathroom, it sounded like someone had been struggling to turn the latch, according to First Post,http://www.first-post.com/living/gaurav-tiwari-indian-ghost-busters-mysterious-death-is-mag-net-for-paranormal-theories-2911340.html. Could it have been Gaurav Tiwari struggling with a malevolent force?

Some say that harmful spirit influences in Mr. Tiwari's life were indeed the factor that either murdered him or caused him to kill himself. Tiwari believed and taught about possible attacks from the spirit world that often left black or blue marks around the neck and other areas of the body. With his combina-tion of spiritual training and scientific knowledge, he was a lifeline for people who felt they were under demonic or spiritual attack, although most of the time the problem the person was experiencing was emotional, not paranormal. For centuries, humans have had unexplained confrontations with the spirit world, leading to injury and sometimes death. It is said that Gaurav Tiwari had been battling a particularly nasty spirit or group of spirits that meant him harm. He had discussed feeling oppressed by a dark spirit, but his family, mostly skeptics, did not take this as meaning that his life was in any danger. On the contrary, he was described as being very involved in his work, but otherwise having an up-beat, yet driven personality.

According to an article in Indian Variety by Deepta Roy Chakaverti, titled "Why I suspect ghosts and demons are behind Gaurav Tiwari's death",http://www.dailyo.in/variety/gaurav-tiwari-bhangarh-fort-ghost-hunter-death-suicide-dark-spirits-rajasthan-haunted-spirits-ghosts-demons/story/1/11720.html, the famous ghost hunters death may be a case of one or more spirits from the 6,000 purportedly haunted sites he visited coming back at him, perhaps seeking revenge. She says that being in certain atmospheres can transfer negative energy, causing a person to become dark and gloomy. Such an example, according to Ms. Chakraverti, is Japan's Aokigahara Forest near the base of Mt, Fuji, also known as "suicide forest" where the forest is the site of many suicides, mostly by hanging from the tall trees that inhabit the forest. Others have claimed that San Francisco's Golden Gate Bridge holds a dark ap-peal to the depressed to end their life. Perhaps, this author notes, the dark ener-gy of Bhangarh Fort stayed hidden during Gaurav Tiwari's visit, only to at-tach to him and drive him to despair and eventually death. She has pho-tographed orbs at the Fort and claims there is more there than meets the eye. The Bhangarh Fort is known to be inhabited by a wizard named Sindhiya, who in life asked a servant to obtain hair oil for the princess Ratnavati whom the wizard loved. The wizard infused the oil with a love potion to obtain the princess's affection. The maid spilled the hair oil on a rock so the wizard cursed the town and is said to still be looking for revenge. Ms. Chakaverti speculates that this haunted place, plus all the others he visited had an effect on his inner being and the energy piled up on him over his years of investigation, only to finally claim him in the end.

Whether you believe in the spirit world or are a total skeptic, one thing for certain is that Gaurav Tiwari made a name for himself by going places that others would avoid at all cost. Right before he died, Tiwari was featured on the cover of Youth Incorporated magazine,

No matter what his cause of death,Gaurav Tiwari made his mark in paranormal research and was responsible for a rise in interest in research and science-based ghost hunting in Asia. He lives on in videos, blog posts and in the hearts of everyone who was lucky enough to be on his team. For now, his branch of the Indian Paranormal Society, GRIP, is on hiatus in mourning for their beloved CEO. The Indian Paranormal Society's website,http://www.indianparanormalsociety.com/, has information about Rev. Tiwari's life and excerpts from his TED Talks, particularly one entitled "Ghosts Are People Too". You can find information about his 6,000 investigations plus the latest news about the society.

CHAPTER FIVE WHAT WE KNOW

Gaurav Tiwari, the 32-year-old paranormal expert and founder-CEO of the Indian Paranormal Society, dedicated his life to investigating bizarre and mysterious events, only to be struck down in death by equally unsettling circumstances. There are conflicting reports and disputed details surrounding the ghost hunter's death. According to family members, he returned home around 1:30 a.m. local time, following a late-night paranormal excursion. Then, he arose a few hours later to practice yoga and bathe. However, the events that followed leading up to his death are suspicious and could be fodder for the Indian Paranormal Society's investigation files.

Some of the family members present at the home claim to have heard signs of a struggle in the bathroom prior to finding Tiwari's Body on the floor that morning. However, apparently, there was no immediate cause for concern until the famed paranormal expert did not emerge from the bathroom. According to reports, Tiwari's wife, Arya, became concerned after her husband failed to exit from the bathroom after an hour. When she attempted to knock on the door, she caught a glimpse of Tiwari's body on the bathroom floor and yelled for help.

Investigators became suspicious of the dark marks found around Tiwari's neck, which lead to an official cause of death of asphyxiation. However, several alternative theories were raised on social media and news reports. While some believe it was a case of auto erotic asphyxiation or possible suicide, others speculate that supernatural forces might have played a role in Tiwari's fate.

There is no denying that the world of the paranormal has its charms and enticements but it also has its pitfalls, especially when there is a morbid fascination or obsession with the dark science that Tiwari built his career and reputation on. In addition to his supernatural pursuits, Tiwari was also an actor, cartoonist, writer, singer, and ordained minister for Metaphysical Church of Humanistic Science (MCHS). Yet, the death of India's most famous paranormal investigator has all the earmarks of suspicious circumstances and could have been featured on his TV show, Bhoot Aaya, which focused on his supernatural endeavors.

WHAT WE KNOW

He was internationally popular in his field, and was featured on July month's cover of Youth Incorporated magazine. He seemed happy posting about it on his Facebook page a day before his death:

Gaurav's father told Times of India that Gaurav complained about some negative energy that was pulling him towards them. Gaurav's father said that his son told this to a daughter in law. However, she had chosen to ignore this.

A day before his death Tiwari was investigating a suspected haunted house in Delhi's Janakpuri area and returned home at around 1.30 a.m. at night.

Preliminary autopsy report suggested asphyxiation as the cause of death. A thin black line across his neck was discovered by the police at the time of death.

His wife, father and mother, were present at home at the time of the incident.

The official cause of death was posted as suicide. This could be the truth, but you will never find supernatural causes as the official cause of death ever anywhere. The only choices that someone who wishes to keep their job is going to be either homicide, suicide or natural causes. This death could have been something else. I leave you to come to your own conclusions.

PARANORMAL INVESTIGATORS 6

HANS HOLZER
THE GHOST HUNTER

By.

Leo Hardy

CHAPTER ONE WHY HANS HOLZER

No history of the world's greatest paranormal investigators would be complete without including Hans Holzer. He will rank as one of the more controversial topics because of some of his over the top claims and the number of books that he penned himself.

It is an interesting fact that he, like the Warrens, investigated the house where what has become known as the Amityville horror took place. It seems that this place attracts paranormal investigators as intensely as it attracts evil. Holzer's investigation of that location and the conclusions that he came to will be the main focus of this book for no other reason that it is the most familiar story to the average reader.

- A ghost is a human being who has passed out of the physical body, usually in a traumatic state and is not aware usually of his true condition. We are all spirits encased in a physical body. At the time of passing, our spirit body continues into the next dimension. A ghost, on the other hand, due to trauma, is stuck in our physical world and needs to be released to go on. — Hans Holzer

Before the Ghost hunters arrived on the sci-fi channel, before anyone heard of Ed and Lorraine Warren there was Hans Holzer. Some said that he was the one who coined the phrase Ghost Hunter. Where ever there was the possibility of a haunting he showed up following a lifelong quest to document the existence of spirits. Hans Holzer was a man who did not like the idea that he was investigating what was referred to as the supernatural, he always considered himself a scientific investigator of the paranormal. So because of this his work in the field put into place the structure by which most modern investigators work.

In this book we are going to examine the career of this brilliant investigator. A career highlighted by his Amityville investigation. Although Ed and Lorraine Warren are more closely associated by the public to this investigation it was Hans Holzer who first attempted to discover the secrets that the Amityville house held. His believe that the crimes committed there were more than just a man murdering his family started an investigation that goes on until today.

There are paranormal investigators that pre-date Hans Holzer, but if there is one person who can be called the godfather of the ghost hunters it is Hans. He wore the title of Ghost Hunter as a badge of honor and because of him millions of people worldwide now take this profession seriously.

Thank you for picking up this book and let's begin with the most obvious question. Since most paranormal investigators are classified as parapsychologist we need to answer first what is parapsychology?

CHAPTER TWO - UNDERSTANDING PARAPSYCHOLOGY

Parapsychology is a field of study concerned with the investigation of paranormal and psychic phenomena.

There are many people that believe in special powers. There are some people that claim to be able to communicate with the dead and even see into the future. Parapsychology is the study of interactions between living things and their environment that seem to surpass the laws of nature. There are five main areas that fall under the study of parapsychology.

Parapsychology looks at telepathy and the way people are able to communicate from mind to mind without verbalizing their thoughts. Some people are said to be able to communicate with others by sharing their thoughts. This field also studies clairvoyance of remote viewing. This means that a person will know objects or people in a different place and a different time. For example a person may be able to know physical features of a room from the past. They can describe exactly what it looked like without any prior knowledge.

Parapsychology also studies precognition which is the knowledge of events and happenings that has not yet occurred or has occurred in the distant past. This information can that be used in the present. A person will be able to future events as well and prepare for these events. Some of them can even see unpleasant things that are said to happen in the future.

People that are able to use parapsychology are able to have psychokinesis where they can interact with things at a distance. This includes interacting with all different types of energy matter. A person can also look at survival studies and examine how the human spirit functions when it is outside of the physical body. This is an interesting field and for many people that believe in this and are willing to find science to support it; this field is interesting to study.

There are some famous parapsychologists who made notable studies in the field. Carlos Alvardo has a PhD in this field and he conducted his research at both the University of Virginia as well as Atlantic University. He would focus on the study of psychic experiences and people that have had these experiences. He also studies psychical research. His research and findings helped him become the President of the Parapsychological Association and his work in this field is still well respected.

Ian Baker is another well-known parapsychologist. He is a professor of Psychology and Parapsychology at the University of Derby. His research and area of expertise is in remote staring. He is also one of the heads of the European Journal of Parapsychology and publishes his research.

John Beloff

Beloff was one of the first people to study parapsychology and make a name for himself in this field. He helped to set up the Koestler Chair of Parapsychology at Edinburgh University. It took a little while for people to take his work seriously but now he is very well respected. He was also the president of the Society for Psychical Research.

Dick J Bierman has a PhD in the field of parapsychology. He shares his knowledge with others at both the University of Utrecht and the University of Amsterdam. He is a physicist as well as a parapsychologist. His research focuses on the relationship between quantum physics and human consciousness. He has been able to develop true random generations to conduct his work. He is also a member of the Global Consciousness Project.

William G Braud

This parapsychologist also has a PhD in the field. He is a professor at the Institute of Psychology which is part of Sofia University. His research focused on the transpersonal psychology as well as parapsychology. He is considered to be an expert on exceptional human experiences, alternative ways of thinking and knowing, and different as well as expanded research methods to really understand the human mind.

Parapsychology is an interesting field of study. Many people are skeptical of dealing with matters that they cannot see and the idea that people can have experiences with other time periods and people that have past. These parapsychologists are conducting research to prove this field is accurate and people are really able to have these experiences. Parapsychology is an interesting field to study and can provide valuable information about how the human brain works and what humans are capable of.

CHAPTER THREE SYBIL LEEK –
WITCH AND PSYCHIC

Sybil Leek was one of the most famous witches in Britain, if not the world. From a young age, Leek wasn't afraid to talk openly about her beliefs, her psychic abilities and the spirits she's encountered. Her fearlessness and eccentric personality made her an unforgettable figure, who would eventually be dubbed "Britain's most famous witch" by the BBC. Prior to her death in 1982, Leek penned more than 60 books about witchcraft and the paranormal and became a well-known public figure, due in part to her collaboration with well-known paranormal investigator Hans Holzer.

Sybil Leek's life reads like a story in itself. From a pet jackdaw to witchy heritage, a highly eccentric family and travels across the world, Leek's life was filled with magic, mystery and spirits from day one.

An Unusual Upbringing

Leek came from comfortable, outwardly ordinary, beginnings. She was born on the 22nd of February 1917 in the little Staffordshire village of Normacot. However, Leek's family was anything but ordinary. In later years Sybil herself claimed ancestry all the way back to Molly Leigh, a famous 16th century witch.

Growing up, Leek was surrounded by believers who thoroughly encouraged her interest in the paranormal. Her immediate family schooled her in topics such as herb craft, divination, psychic skills, nature and more. While other youngsters could look forward to visits from prim aunts or the local vicar, Leek's home played host to such characters as Aleister Crowley and H G Wells.

The White Witch

By 1950, Leek was living in the New Forest, an area steeped in folklore and mystery. Leek would later say that she had contact with the New Forest witches and deepened her craft with them. After a vision in the woods told Leek that the psychic arts and old magic were her destiny, she began to publicly proclaim herself as a white witch.

The witchcraft act in Britain wasn't repealed until 1951, making Leek's audacious claims both bold and brave. With her eccentric manner and openness about her psychic craft, Leek soon began to attract the attention of the world's media.

Leaving England

Leek's growing fame wasn't entirely comfortable. Although her home village benefited from increased tourism and attention, Leek herself soon began to tire of the media attention. Her contemporaries at the time accused her of being a fraud, or simply a joke, and the time soon came for Leek to take her psychic career across the water.

When her landlord refused to renew her lease, Leek took it as a sign to move on, and traveled to America to begin work as an astrologer. Leek couldn't have known at the time (or perhaps she could!) but this move would introduce her to her greatest collaborator, Hans Holzer.

A Meaningful Encounter

In 1964, Leek was invited to appear on the American television show To Tell The Truth, in order to talk about her new book, A Shop In The High Street. While in New York for the interview, Leek was invited to meet noted parapsychologist Hans Holzer, and a dream team was born.

Hans Holzer had spent his life interested in the weird and wonderful. Born in Austria in 1920, Holzer became interested in the paranormal at a young age, and dedicated his life to studying the unseen. He wrote over 100 books on the subject, and although he is best known for his work on the Amityville case, his interest in psychic subjects was wide and deep. He became interested in the white witch of England, and he and Leek soon began to work together.

Working Together

Leek and Holzer soon established a strong working relationship. The pair would travel near and far investigating psychic and paranormal cases that had come to Holzer's attention. Their work soon attracted interest from both local and national media who were fascinated by the eccentric psychic and her collaborator.

Holzer was in charge of choosing the cases they investigated, based on the criteria that each had the potential to become a solid psychic case which provided interesting material or evidence. Leek was never privy to where they were going or what they were investigating next, as Holzer didn't want her work to be colored by prior knowledge or assumptions. As a result, Leek never knew where her work with Holzer would take her next.

When they reached the site of an investigation, Leek had no trouble slipping into a trance and bringing through a wealth of information, which Holzer would then work with and attempt to substantiate.

From Coast To Coast

Leek and Holzer traveled through many locations in their work. On one occasion, they visited the Greenwich Village home of actress June Havoc, who was being terrorized by a ghost. Leek was able to connect with the spirit, who would come to be known as Hungry Lucy, a Revolutionary-era girl who was cold and starving. Throughout the course of several séances, Lucy eventually moved peacefully to the other side.

The duo also investigated the well-known Whaley House in California. Leek connected with the spirit of Mr. Whaley, who was angry at perceived injustices towards himself and his house. She also communicated with the spirit of a Russian man who had died in the area while hunting sea otters; the Russian presence in the area at the time was a very little known fact, adding weight to Leek's story.

Over the course of their work together, Leek and Whaley investigated many hauntings, and appeared on many TV and radio shows on the subject. In later years Leek moved to Florida, where she continued to speak extensively in both America and Britain. She finally passed away on the 26th of October, 1982.

Sybil Leek was an eccentric and unforgettable figure; passionate about her craft and about astrology, outspoken, often at odds with other witches, and unafraid to practice and talk of her psychic craft to anyone who was willing to listen.

CHAPTER FOUR AMITYVILLE

Amityville as a town and the Amityville Horror that happened in quaint little town are of both legend and a horrible reality that the world over has heard of and probably knows well. The legend has brought about many inconsistencies and far-fetched rumors so that movies can be made to make money from the terrible reality of what really happened there. The truth about the Amityville Horror has been written by more than one individual.

Probably the most well-known writer on this subject is Hans Holzer. He involved himself deeply in the investigation and the legend in order to decipher the truth from the myths. When looking at the facts around the case, the truth is far scarier than fiction could ever be. Those that say the truth is not accurate are just scared to admit that these things are truly possible and completely real. The Amityville Horror was one of the first true hauntings that brought about psychics and paranormal investigators to dig deep into investigations to educate the public.

The Amityville Horror happened at 112 Ocean Avenue in Amityville, New York. The demonic evil presence inhabited Ronald DeFeo in 1974 when he killed his entire family, which was one year prior to December of 1975 when the Lutz family bought the Amityville house. The parents and three children moved into the house and did not stay very long. They stayed in the house for one month and then fled the haunted house.

Ed and Lorraine Warren are two paranormal investigators who investigated the happenings at the Amityville house and wrote a detailed article on the demonic evil haunting. Some say the house was possessed and some say that the family itself was possessed the presence. Ed and Lorraine are two out of nine people that have investigated the Amityville legend. The Warrens and a man named Dr. Kaplan have been battling this issue out for many years. They are on completely opposite ends of the issue. The proof of the facts is always going to be debatable. The only solid truth is that something evil and demonic did indeed happen there, but there is no one that lived with the presence that will be able to once and for all clear up the confusion on the Amityville case.

The absolute truth is often hard to come by, especially with paranormal investigations because so many do not believe in the ghosts and demonic presences in the world and some do. Possession is mainly from personal interpretation. Myths and interpretations tend to get out of hand and bring about too many different stories for people to ingest. It is hard to know what is real or legend because so much has been written on the Amityville horror. Trying to find the 100% authentic story on the subject is like looking for a needle in a haystack. The hunt for the truth will always be going on because for some people this kind of investigating will be life-long pursuit. I'm sure that someone will dig deep enough to figure out the real deal.

CHAPTER FIVE HANS HOLZER

With the recent movie fame that Hollywood has given to ghost hunters Ed and Lorraine Warren, people don't realize that before the Warren's began, Hans Holzer had already been crowned the King of the paranormal investigators. Between his investigation into the infamous Amityville house, and more than 140 published books on ghosts and the afterlife, he definitely earned that title.

Hans Holzer was born in Vienna, Austria on January 26, 1920. Holzer attended the University of Vienna where he studied ancient history, numismatics, and archaeology. In 1938, just before the Nazi takeover, Holzer's family felt it was unsafe to remain in Austria and left the country to settle down in New York City. Once in New York, Holzer attended Columbia University where he studied Japanese. He then went on to earn a master's degree in comparative religion, and a doctorate in parapsychology at the London College of Applied Science. After obtaining his PhD, he began teaching parapsychology at the New York Institution of Technology. Describing himself as an academic parapsychologist, he took his work very seriously.

There were three words that according to Holzer, were "dirty words" to him. Belief, disbelief, and supernatural. To him, belief were ideas that could not be supported by fact and supernatural implied that paranormal phenomena was the beyond the reach of science. He did not believe in religion and thought of the concept as corporations using the idea of religion to make a profit by scaring their followers. He even gave up celebrating Christmas after being convinced that Jesus was born on October 3, 7BC. He was quoted saying "If it weren't for parapsychology, religion wouldn't have a leg to stand on."

Holzer's interest in the paranormal began at a very young age, after hearing stories on the subject from his uncle. He was a firm believer in life after death and began to explore the existence of ghosts, spirits, and what he named the "stay behinds" by investigating haunted houses and having conversations with those who believed that they had experienced paranormal happenings. He didn't like to use any electronic gadgets for detecting cold spots, anomalies, or to contact spirits. Instead, he preferred using a medium to make direct communication. According to him, spirits were imprints left behind which could be picked up by sensitive people.

During his investigations into the paranormal world, he began traveling the world to various haunted places, uncovering the paranormal in New Hampshire, Connecticut and even a haunted train in Switzerland. The most famous of these places was located at 112 Ocean Avenue on the south shore of Long Island in Amityville, New York. In December 1975, the Lutz family moved into the house. After only 28 days, they vacated the premises. They claimed to have been tormented by something paranormal in that house.

Thirteen months prior to the Lutz family moved in, the house had been the scene of multiple murders. Ronald DeFeo Jr. brutally murdered his parents and four siblings by going room to room, shooting each one of them while they slept. Following the reports of a paranormal activity from the Lutz family, the Amityville house was explored by Holzer along with a spiritual medium named Ethel Johnson-Meyers in 1977. Ethel claimed that Defeo Jr. had been possessed by the spirit of a Shinnecock Indian by the name of Chief Rolling Thunder, and that the house had been built on top of an ancient Native American burial ground. Photos that were taken at the scene showed mysterious halos in the images of bullet marks made in the 1974 murders. Holzer went on to write several books based on his findings. His non-fiction book "Murder in Amityville" was published in 1979. He also wrote the novels "The Amityville Curse", published in 1981, and "The Secret of Amityville", published in 1985.

Throughout all of his paranormal investigations, Holzer was never afraid. On the television series In Search Of, he told Leonard Nimoy "In all my years of ghost hunting, I have never been afraid. After all, a ghost is only a fellow human being in trouble." He believed that spirits could be people who did not realize they were dead, and are therefore "confused as to their real status." Apart from his beliefs in ghosts, he was convinced in the existence of extraterrestrial life and that they had been abducting humans to learn about life on earth. He also spoke about reincarnation. He had recollections of himself being present at the Battle of Glencoe in 1692, being a Wiccan high priest, and a vegan in past lives. Holzer had actually been a vegetarian since age 11 and a vegan since his early 40s.

Hans Holzer remains the world's most famous paranormal investigators. He wrote well over 100 books on ghosts, paranormal phenomena, the occult, UFOs and extraterrestrials, and psychic healing. Some of his most notable works include, "Ghosts I've Met" (1965), "Yankee Ghosts" (1966), "Hans Holzer's Haunted Houses: A Pictorial Register of the World's Most Interesting Ghost Houses" (1971), "Haunted Hollywood" (1974), "Ghosts of New England: True Stories of Encounters With the Phantoms of New England and New York." (1989), "The Directory of Psychics: How to Find, Evaluate, and Communicate with Professional Psychics and Mediums" (1995), and "Witches: True Encounters with Wicca, Wizards, Covens, Cults, and Magick" (2002). He was also a frequent guest on television talk shows, and even hosted "Ghost Hunter", his own show.

Hans Holzer passed on into the world he spent his whole life studying on April 26, 2009 in New York City, NY. He is survived by his two daughters from his marriage to Countess Catherine Genevieve Buxhoeveden, a descendant of Catherine "The Great", along with his five grandchildren. In an interview with www.ghostvillage.com, Holzer was asked how he wanted to be remembered. He replied by saying, "As a man who told the truth. I won't have a tombstone. Cemeteries are real estate wastes, and I don't believe in funerals of any kind. The sooner you burn the body the better. It's just a shell. Mankind has a lot to learn." May we all learn from your work, Mr. Holzer.

PARANORMAL INVESTIGATORS 7

The Werewolf and the Demon Trial
An Ed and Lorraine Warren File

By.
Rodney C. Cannon and Leo Hardy

CHAPTER ONE THE DEMONOLOGIST

What is a Demonologist?

Introduction

Demonology is essentially the study of demons and the belief system that surrounds them. Theologically speaking it relates to supernatural beings that are more powerful than humans but still far beneath gods within many different mythologies. Unlike its name implies however it does not focus solely on malevolent beings the kind of which are depicted in film and on television, but also with benevolent beings that have few if any worshipers and are as such not very well known. To the thinking of many people, demons are dark, malignant spirits that hearken to a much darker lifestyle and are meant to torment the living. While this is might be in part quite accurate, it is not the only focus of a demonologist.

What A Demonologist Does

The word "demon" at one time meant a benevolent being, but its translation to English somehow switched that meaning to something far darker and less kind. When regarded as spirits, demons are often thought of as discarnate souls that have never had a body of their own. This however depends on the myths of each culture in which demons appear. If one was to look at the myths and legends surrounding demons in Africa as opposed to America they might find that one culture believes in demons as spiritual beings without a body of their own, whereas the popular myth of the day in America is that demons can either possess a body, or are possessed of their own grotesque, unholy form. Whatever culture you go to demons are more often than not seen as rather dark beings, no matter the origin of their label. Demonology, though considered a pseudoscience by many, has been a prevalent influence throughout many cultures. There have been a great many societies that have believed in the existence of spirits both benevolent and malignant, and demons have at times been an easy target for the woes of mankind when things begin to go wrong. Most people would assume that a demonologist is one who summons demons or perhaps banishes them much like you would see in "The Exorcist". Unfortunately this is not entirely accurate, as a demonologist is not a position that many within the Christian faith would seek to cling to. Not only is a means by which to endanger yourself and others, it is a calling to which few are drawn, and one which relies heavily upon the presence of God and all His blessings to stay safe, and sane. Demons are reputed to be very real, though also very selective in who they choose to torment. The role of a demonologist is to study and understand those spirits who mean to bring harm and torment to others. They are not always priests, but they are most always Christians who have fully accepted God into their lives for protection. The glitz and glamour of demonologists relying heavily on the holy bible as seen in the movies is more for show than any historical accuracy when it comes to the study of demonology.

Psalm 106:37-38 - "They sacrificed their sons and their daughters to the demons; they poured out innocent blood, the blood of their sons and daughters, whom they sacrificed to the idols of Canaan, and the land was polluted with blood." -

Demonologist vs. Ghost Hunter

Many people would lump a demonologist, or paranormal investigator as many of them are known, into the same group as a ghost hunter. This is a common misconception that tends to generalize the far more intricate life of a demonologist. While the ghost hunter is out seeking proof positive of spirits that exist in haunted houses, forests, and various other regions, the demonologist investigates the possibility that a spirit exists in such locations. Ghost hunters are continually on the prowl to find one ghost after another, thinking only to find their "prey" as the term "hunter" would imply. Once they have found what they are seeking they tend to move on, the thrill of finding ghosts spurring them ever onward. Demonologists on the other hand are labeled as investigators, as in they seek out mentions and hints of spirits but do not actively engage unless there is no other choice. The life of a demonologist is said to be quite lonely as they devote much of their time and effort to their studies and tend to eschew any other type of relationship to others. Demons are said to inhabit any living specimen they can, and the presence of loved ones, even pets, can grant too much of a weakness to any living soul should a demon find it necessary to torment them. Demonologists are quite simply those who study the paranormal and, if necessary, take note of how it affects humanity and employ those who are trained in such arts to keep any who are affected from harm.

Conclusion

Demons are defined by the Western world and many other cultures as malevolent, harmful spirits that are bent on destroying the race of mankind. They are said to be devious, deceitful, and capable of out-thinking and outwitting even the smartest human alive, and as such are considered extremely dangerous. Those who have risked their lives and their sanity to divine the nature of demons have often placed themselves on the front lines of the unseen war that rages beyond the reckoning of human beings, watching and observing in order to better understand what is not seen. Demonologists are not the holy water-packing religious warriors from the movies, but are still very aware of the spiritual realm that exists just beyond the human sphere.

CHAPTER TWO THE WARRENS AND THE GLAZEL FAMILY

- **"Diabolical forces are formidable. These forces are eternal, and they exist today. The fairy tale is true. The devil exists. God exists. And for us, as people, our very destiny hinges upon which one we elect to follow. - Ed Warren**

While some people believe that such things as demonic possession can and do occur, others are not so certain. Still others don't buy into it at all, no matter how much evidence seems to support a particular story. With that being said, you can read the following article and then draw your own conclusions. Who knows, you might even be tempted to conduct some further research regarding the story in order to make a well-educated determination that is completely based on your own findings.

Background Information

Whatever your personal beliefs might be, this particular story is one that is based on events that actually occurred, or at least that is what the individuals that were involved claim. It involves the rather famous individuals Ed and Lorraine Warren, a couple that were self-proclaimed demonologists and are best known for working on the case that later became famous in the movie, The Amityville Horror. Even this particular story has been recounted several times, both in print and for television. Of course, every time the story is told the person telling it has a tendency to put their own spin on things by changing a few things or leaving some information out altogether, such as was the case when the story was depicted on the popular television series A Haunting. Regardless of that fact, it centers around the Glatzel family, namely their 11 year old son David. Supposedly, David was possessed by a demon and this position eventually led to a murder being committed by another individual who claimed to have later been affected by the same demon.

How It All Began

During the early 1980s, the Glatzel family was moving into a new home in New England. The couple and their 11 year old son David were getting the house ready when they realized that things had been left inside of it from the previous tenants. In fact, even the beds had been left in place, almost as if the individuals who lived there before them had been in a rush to get out. However, the family didn't think much of it and proceeded to go about cleaning up the house so that they could move their things in and get settled. Almost immediately, David noticed that something wasn't quite right, especially when he went to clean up one of the back bedrooms. According to his recollection of the story, he was approached by an old man that actually shoved him and then disappeared. Obviously, this would be enough to scare anyone and scare him it did. He spent the rest of the afternoon outside in the front yard, refusing to have anything more to do with the house. Despite that fact, the family was determined to make the house their new home so he eventually had no choice but to go back inside. Despite the fact that he told his parents what happened and that even they were hearing rather strange noises in the attic, they really didn't know what to make of it at first and they thought that it had a lot more to do with his overactive imagination than anything else.

Escalating Events

Over a rather short amount of time, events escalated to the point that the boy was not only seeing visions, but also going into a trance-like state where he would often not appear to be himself. He would even talk in a voice that was not his own. Eventually, his desperate parents contacted the Warrens in an attempt to get to the bottom of things. According to their version of events, he predicted things that were yet to occur, but did occur as predicted at a later time. He also seemed to have a way of knowing things that happened when he was nowhere around and according to Lorraine Warren, he even went into a trance and levitated right in front of her. She also claimed that she could see a dark mist that was hovering around him and that she could sense a very evil presence. Eventually, the Warrens arranged for an exorcism. Unsuccessful on the first attempt, it eventually required at least two more exorcisms and a blessing of the house before young David could have any semblance of a normal life. Unfortunately, both the Glatzel family and the Warrens contend that when the demon left David's body, it entered the body of another individual that was nearby, namely Arne Cheyenne Johnson.

The Murder

By this time, the family had decided to have nothing more to do with the home and moved out, eventually finding an apartment that was rented by the employer of David's mother, Alan Bono. According to all of the parties involved, she was working as a dog groomer for him and her family was living in the apartment. However, it became clear that Johnson was possessed as strange things started to happen inside the apartment as well. According to some accounts, this occurred after Johnson visited the home where the events initially occurred and found a well in the backyard, supposedly coming face-to-face with the demon. The Warrens also claimed that they were so concerned that something was going to happen that they contacted the local authorities in an attempt to warn them and prevent anything from happening in the first place. Despite these claims, the official account is that Bono and the family were eating lunch together and then Bono had gotten drunk, eventually confronting Johnson's wife and physically preventing her from leaving the building. Johnson, who had been dealing with rage building up inside of him for weeks, pulled out a knife and stabbed Bono several times, resulting in his death at a hospital several hours after the attack occurred. These events occurred on February 16th, 1981.

The Conviction

On November 24th, 1981 Johnson found himself being convicted in court in Brookfield, Connecticut. Facing a first-degree manslaughter charge, he was ultimately convicted because the judge determined that it was not possible to positively ascertain whether or not any individual is possessed by a demon or if they are acting on their own accord. Unable to prove otherwise beyond a shadow of a doubt, he was ultimately sent to prison. However, it is important to note that out of the original term, which carried a prison sentence of 10 to 20 years, he served only 5 and was then released. To this day, he claims that he himself had nothing to do with the murder and that he was not acting out of his own free will when it occurred. Instead, he claims that he was possessed by a demon and that it was in total control throughout the event.

Conclusion

Is it possible to the decide with complete and total certainty that Johnson was indeed possessed or that any of this actually occurred in the first place? The truth is, there is really not enough evidence to prove it beyond a shadow of a doubt, especially as far as the courts are concerned. However, everyone that was involved in these events has always maintained that they were being completely truthful and honest and that they themselves saw more than enough proof with their own eyes. What do you think really happened?

CHAPTER THREE THE DEMON POSSESSION TRIAL

Demons, paranormal activity, and ghost. Do they really exist? There are many books, movies, and television shows that depict individuals who are possessed or claim to have witnessed paranormal activity. There has been one instance where this subject has come to attention in a court of law.

Ed and Lorraine Warren would be ones to tell us that paranormal activity is indeed a real occurrence. They based their livelihood off doing so. They are famous demonologist who are most known for the work they have done regarding the infamous Amityville horrors. The husband and wife worked on very high profile cases and have investigated over ten thousand paranormal cases throughout their careers. One of those cases included the trial of Arne Johnson.

The trial of Arne Cheyenne Johnson was a truly unique case. One that people still discuss thirty years later and will continue to discuss for years to come. The trial is the first trial in history that claims and attempts to prove that a demon was responsible for the actions of the defendant.

In 1981, at the young age of 19, Arne Cheyenne Johnson was arrested and charged with first degree manslaughter for the murder of his landlord, Alan Bono. In the midst of a heated argument between the two, Johnson pulled out a pocketknife and stabbed Bono repeatedly. Johnson lived in a small town where murder was an anomaly. It was the first murder that occurred in Brookline, Connecticut. The small town was shocked to its core.

Johnson was living with his girlfriend Debbie Glatzel. Her brother, David Glatzel, was said to be experiencing paranormal activity. His family believed that he had a demon living inside him, tormenting him. The Glatzel family became worried and sought help for the child. The family called on the best to try and help David become a normal child once again.

Ed and Lorraine Warren were called upon to help David get rid of the demon living inside him. The Warrens, along with several priest, began the mission of removing the demons from David. There were several exorcisms performed. The process lasted for days. There are claims that there were numerous demons living inside of David. Arne Johnson believed that the demons that were exorcised from David began to take up residence inside of his body.

Only a month after witnessing the demons being exorcised from David, Johnson then murdered his landlord during a heated argument. Johnson had no prior criminal history, nor did he have a history of violent behavior.

Ed and Lorraine Warren claimed that David was possessed and they witnessed the demon actually leaving David's body. They were positive that the demons were now inside of Johnson. They advocated on behalf of Arne Johnson. They went to the police to inform them of the demons living inside of Johnson, claiming that Johnson was not responsible for his actions. If there were not demons living inside of him, he would never have committed a murder in his life.

The trial began to take on a life of its own. Never before had anyone heard of something like this. Murder by demon. Everyone was intrigued. There was no doubt that the Warrens had a lot to do with the sensationalizing of this case. During the trial, people all over the world were trying to learn about the case. The defense attorney was bombarded with calls throughout the trial. It became known as the "Devil Made me do it" case. It was also known as the "Demon Murder Trial".

The trial proceedings began in October of 1981. The defense attempted to enter a plea of not guilty by reason of possession. The judge refused to allow this plea. The judge felt that there was no way to prove this in a court of law. There was no real evidence that could be proven. Johnson was convicted of first degree manslaughter and sentenced to ten to twenty years in jail. He only served five.

The real drama came after the trial. The case led to movie and book deals due to the Warren's work on this case. Gerald Brittle wrote the book, "The Devil in Connecticut", with the help of Lorraine Warren. The family went on to say that they were being exploited by the Warren's and sued them. The Glatzel family claimed that the Warren's told them that their story could make them millionaire's if they shared it with the world. The Warren's believe that the family is suing for monetary purposes only.

CHAPTER FOUR THE WEREWOLF THE FACTS

-Even a man who is pure in heart And says his prayers by night May become a wolf when the wolfs bane blooms

And the autumn moon is bright - The Wolfman

Werewolves,men who have the fortune or misfortune to become wolves or half-wolf, half-men creatures, have existed in human culture since the 1st century AD. Werewolves or lycanthropy, the power to transform into werewolves, became widespread in literature from the 15th and 16th centuries onward, at first through the documentation of those who behaved in a wolf-like manner or imagined themselves to be wolves. Often, the transformation is triggered by moonlight or a full moon. From there, the werewolf in fiction thrived, eventually becoming sometimes heroic rather than always evil, and gaining unique attributes—e.g. weakness against silver bullets—and even sex appeal.

Lycanthropy as a Mental Illness

Those who believe they are real-life werewolves, however, don't lead glamorous lives. In modern medicine, they would generally be diagnosed with clinical lycanthropy, a loosely defined form of psychosis in which patients feel like wolves, believe they are turning into wolves, or act like wolves. Some experts also suggest schizophrenia or bipolar disorder as the cause. Others might well ask if there is more to lycanthropy than simple delusions: after all, the idea that the moon can drive people mad long predates werewolves. The English word "lunacy"—which evolved from the Latin "lunaticus"—is based on the thought that the phases of the moon, the luna, can cause periods of insanity. According to research published in the British Medical Journal (Clinical Research Edition),crime rates increase when there is a full moon, possible because of gravitational effects on "human tidal waves." Could it be that the moon causes the inner selves of susceptible or already afflicted individuals to transform into wolves?

Lycanthropy as a Physical Illness

It may be difficult to believe lycanthropy exists only within the mind, considering the number of supposed sightings and attacks documented throughout history. As with vampires, werewolves are sometimes believed to be actually people suffering from untreated rabies, as noted in The Werewolf Delusion. Symptoms of rabies include itching, headache, delirium, and abnormal behavior, according to the Centers for Disease Control and Prevention. In advanced stages, symptoms include increased salivation, muscle spasms in the throat and larynx, and fear of water, i.e. hydrophobia.Rabies may also spread to the spine, causing weakness or dysfunction of the limbs. In an era before electric street lights, it's easy to see how someone suffering from delirium, paranoia, and pain, perhaps crying out unintelligibly and stumbling about—even on all fours—while frothing at the mouth may have appeared as a wolf man. This was, after all, when wolves roamed most regions and were a top carrier for the rabies virus. The delirious person might also mistake the moon or moonlight for the reflection of light on water, which can worsen the symptoms of hydrophobia. A similar explanation is erythropoietic porphyria, a disease that causes excessive hair, reddish teeth, and a fear of light, according to the Public Library of Science.

The Werewolf Syndrome

If scientific explanations are what you seek, rabies may be less straightforward than hypertrichosis, also known as Ambras syndrome or werewolf syndrome. Patients grow excessive hair that is longer and thicker than normal, often on the face or the full body. In the past, those who suffer from this incurable disease were seen as part-human, part-some other animal, and although hypertrichosis would have been much rarer than rabies even then, one could easily imagine these misunderstood, misaligned individuals hunting for food on the outskirts of villages and towns and keeping their wolf-like faces or bodies hidden during daytime. The bolder of these "werewolves" hired themselves out as circus attractions or novelties for the upper classes, as with the likes of Petrus Gonzales, Jesus Aceves,and Julia Pastrana, according to Scientific American.Because this rare genetic disorder affects men more than women, it also makes sense that werewolves are almost always depicted as males.

The Supernatural

If you reject science-based explanations of werewolves, you'd be pleased to know that numerous ancient cultures spoke of possessed men who take on the abilities and behavior of wolves. In Scandinavian legend, for instance, two men under the possession of enchanted wolf skins began to kill people they encountered in the woods, as noted in the Encyclopedia Britannica. South America lore mentions boys transform into wolves under the influence of the full moon. In Mexico, lycanthropy was less a curse than a magical power, while in Germany, both fairy tales and historical accounts described people accused of lycanthropy with the aid of magical items. The University of Pittsburgh documents many German tales of werewolves, often involving magical belts or pelts. What all these stories have in common is the portrayal of the werewolf as cruel and evil, with most suggesting lycanthropy is an unwanted possession by dark magic rather than a gift of supernatural powers.

From a probabilistic standpoint, one might argue that a combination of all of the above explanations is more likely than any single one. Since most of these causes are also incurable, perhaps it's less important to ask why people claim to be or are accused of being werewolves—perhaps it's more important to acknowledge that werewolves may have always walked among us.

CHAPTER FIVE THE WEREWOLF OF LONDON, BILL RAMSEY

There have been tales of monsters and demonic presences and possessions for as long as men have told stories; there have also been crimes, and people who would do or say anything to escape prosecution for those crimes. While it was not uncommon in previous centuries for demons or monsters to be blamed for unexplained or particularly violent crimes; with the medical, psychological and sociological advances of today's society, blaming said demons or monsters for the works of a disturbed mind seems far-fetched at best. So, in the 1983 case of William Ramsey, the international story or the Werewolf of Southend, was Bill Ramsey really possessed by a demonic werewolf presence, or were he and others involved in his case playing on the fears of the populace?

Case Background

In 1983 in Southend, Essex, UK, Bill Ramsey checked himself into a hospital with severe chest pains; and later, after he attacked Emergency Room nurses and was transferred to a mental hospital and then released, Ramsey turned himself into police. He asked that he be locked up for his own safety and for the safety of others, but before he could be shown to a cell, reports show that he attacked the attending officer and was forcibly sedated and placed in a cell. After a report of the incident went international, self proclaimed demonologists Ed and Lorraine Warren traveled from America to England to investigate the case, as they believed it could be a case of possession by a demonic werewolf spirit. The Warrens took Ramsey back to America with them where they and assisting priests and doctors performed an exorcism of Bill Ramsey after which Ramsey was proclaimed cured and he returned home to his family, never to have werewolf life urges again.

Controversy

Was Bill Ramsey indeed possessed by a demonic werewolf spirit, or was he simply suffering from a diminished mental capacity which left him predisposed to commit violent crimes? Either way, it is unclear whether Bill Ramsey served any sentence or was even prosecuted in the first place for his attacks on nurses, police officers and other innocent bystanders. Was Bill Ramsey cured, or did he see a get-out-of-jail free card in exploiting the beliefs of the Warrens? Is there sufficient, conclusive evidence to show that Ramsey was not just an exceptionally intelligent and twisted individual?

Demonic Possession

As a child, all records indicate Bill Ramsey was a normal, active and imaginative little boy who loved to play. He would run around the backyard of his parents' home in Southend, using his imagination to fight wrongdoers and save the damsel in distress. He always played the hero, doing good and ridding the world of evil were among his favorite pass times. Then one day, everything changed. When Ramsey was nine years old, records indicate as he was romping among his mother's clean laundry when he was suddenly overcome with cold chills and strange feelings of an out of body experience. Ramsey says he no longer felt human, but was hen an enraged wolf full of bloodlust. In his fit of animalistic violence, reports indicate nine year old Ramsey pulled a fence post out of the ground and began to swing it about before ripping it apart with his hands and teeth, scaring his parents so that they fled into their home and locked their child out. After a short time, Ramsey just as suddenly reverted back to his original state of mind, claiming no recollection of the events of the afternoon. For fifteen years, it seemed that afternoon would remain an isolated incident. Then Ramsey says he began having nightmares in which his wife would flee from the sight of him and when he woke cold and shaky from the repeating nightmares, Ramsey claimed he could hear a wild animal howling somewhere in his home, only to realize that it was himself making the noises. Again, Ramsey went fifteen years without another incident, and then it seems several incidents happened in quick succession. In a matter of months, Ramsey attacked friends after a night of partying, ER nurses as he was being examined after feeling chest pains, and a police officer after turning himself in, frightened that he would attack someone. Therefore, the question is, did Bill Ramsey experience demonic possession; or, did he lose control and go on a rampage, and then use demonic possession ass scapegoat to escape punishment for his crimes? Various reports have been found on the subject, but remain as different and inconclusive in the detailing as they are numerous.

Clinical Lycanthropy

Some reports indicate that, as a child, Ramsey suffered from violent seizures with left him writhing and howling in agony, lashing out at those around him. As it has been suggested that seizures lead to diminished mental capacity, it is not a far leap to claim that the seizures did indeed cause the diminished mental capacity that led Ramsey to believe he was, and therefore act like, a werewolf. His description of sudden onset of cold chills followed by intense emotions and lack of memory are all signs of side effects of seizures. Even his body movements can be attributed to the kinds of seizures that cause a person's body to spasm out of control. The account fifteen years later of his recurring nightmares, cold chills and howling could once again be contributed to seizures. It is not uncommon for a person to experience severe seizures few and far between if and when they are exposed to certain stimuli. Arguably, the same could be said for the 1983 incidents that led to the involvement of American Demonologists.

After the involvement of Demonologists Ed and Lorraine Warren, Ramsey was said to be cured of his ailment and returned home to his family. It is said that he never again suffered an episode of violence, and it remains unclear if he was prosecuted for the crimes committed during his states of incapacity.

For all of the ghost hunters, poltergeist experts and demonologists in today's society, little more is known or understood now of demons and monsters than when they were supposedly running rampant through the countryside, to blame for every unexplained terrible accident or crime. The fact that so little is known of the subject makes it even harder to believe or accept that demonic possessions instead of mental illnesses could be to blame for the actions of a disturbed individual. As for the case of Bill Ramsey, the Werewolf of Southend, reports and conclusions of what actually happened are still as inconclusive today as they were thirty years ago, leaving no definitive answer as to what really happened in England all those years ago.

PARANORMAL INVESTIGATORS BOOK 8

HARRY HOUDINI AND SIR ARTHUR CONAN DOYLE

By.

Leo Hardy

CHAPTER ONE HARRY HOUDINI

I am a great admirer of mystery and magic. Look at this life - all mystery and magic. Harry Houdini

Who was Harry Houdini?

The man Harry Houdini is known by many people all over the world as the best magician to have ever lived. He's known to be among the top pioneers of modern magic. Harry was born on March 24th, 1874 Hungary in Budapest. His real name was Erich Weisz. He moved to Appleton with his family at a young age.

Young Harry was always fascinated with magic and immediately began to perform in small shows. At the age of 20, he married his wife. Wilhelmina Rahner, who also became his apprentice in the world of magic. Harry performed escape magic acts all his life until he died at 52.

Early life

Erich Weisz was born in Budapest, Hungary on the 24th of March 1874. Harry Houdini was a son of a Jewish rabbi who with his other 6 siblings lived in one house. As a child, they moved to Appleton, Wisconsin with his whole family. When Harry turned 13, he moved with his father to New York where they took odd jobs so as to fend for themselves. The rest of the family later joined them. It was at this period where Harry became fully interested in the Trapeze arts.

Erich Weisz launched officially his magician career in 1894 as a full-time magician where he named himself Harry Houdini. The name Harry had been derived from his childhood name, Ehrie and yet the last from as homage to great magician Jean Houdini. He slowly but gradually drew the attention of many due to his shows of handcuffs escapes. In 1893, Harry married his fellow performer Wilhelmina Rahner, who served as Harry's' lifelong stage partner and assistant under a stage name of "Bess" Houdini.

Houdini's Commercial Success

In 1899, Harry Houdini's magical act caught Martin Becks' attention who was an entertainment manager who almost instantly got him booked at among the best venues for magic performances all over the country. He did a tour even to Europe. He was slowly making a name for himself with the feats. Houdini's feats at times even involved the local town police, who after strip searching him, would place him in heavy shackles and properly lock him inside their jails, only later discovering that he had managed somehow to escape. His shows were always a huge sensation, with massive crowds turning up to his shows whenever he traveled. He soon rose up the ranks to become the most-paid magic performer in the whole of American vaudeville.

Exploits Outside of Magic

Harry Houdini's wealth had allowed him to also indulge in other passions that he loved, such as film and aviation. He bought his first plane in 1909 and also set out to be the first person to man a controlled flight over Australia in 1910. While he finally did it going through a few failed attempts, it was known that Houdini was beaten by just some months by Capt. Colin Defries, who had made a short plane flight in December 1909.

Houdini launched also his movie career in 1901 when he released the 1st film, the "Merveilleux Exploits du Célébre Houdini Paris", that documented all his escapes. He appeared in several films, including The Grim Game, The Master Mystery and Terror Island. At New York, Harry started began own film company and also a film lab even though none was a success. In 1923, Houdini was made the president of Martinka & Co, which is America's oldest magic company.

As the president of the company of American Magicians, Houdini was known as a vigorous campaigner against fraudulent mediums. He even debunked Mina Crandon a renowned medium, who was commonly known as Margery. The act automatically turned him against his former ally Sir Arthur Conan Doyle, who was a great believer in spiritualism and Margery's acts. Despite all his activism that stood against spiritualism, Harry and his wife did experiment with spiritualism when they decided that whoever died first among them would try to establish a communication from the grave with the living person. Well, before her death in 1943, Beatrice, declare this impossible and the experiment was a failure.

Houdini's Mysterious Death

Even though there are a number mixed reports explaining Harry's' cause of death it only certain that he had suffered for quite a while from acute appendicitis. Whether his suffering was brought about by a University student punched him in the stomach as some sort of testing or by a poison he got from a group of angered Spiritualists is still unknown. What is certainly known is that Harry died due to a ruptured appendix at the age of 52 on 31st of October 1926, in Detroit, Michigan.

CHAPTER TWO
HOUDINI AND SPIRITUALISM

Turning to Spiritualism After the Death of Cecilia Weiss

Harry Houdini is actually famous for debunking mystical claims. As such, the fact that he was actually interested in finding evidence for life after death might be interesting to a lot of people. Harry Houdini's journey as a ghost hunter began with the death of his mother Cecilia Weiss. Cecilia seemed to have had a neutral attitude towards ghosts and spirits while she was alive, which was common during this time period. Skepticism towards ghosts is more common today, and it was less common at this point in time.

She didn't seem to have been much of an enthusiast for the supernatural, either as someone who loved it or as someone who feared it. However, Cecilia was extremely close to Harry Houdini and to his wife Bess. Like many people who turn to the study of ghosts and spirits, Harry Houdini was primarily motivated by grief. Cecilia Weiss died in 1913, and Harry Houdini was a ghost hunter on a mission from that point onward.

Harry Houdini and Spiritualism

Spiritualism had been very popular for nearly a century by the time Harry Houdini started to get interested in it. People throughout the nineteenth century and the twentieth century were often trying to find out differing belief systems as a number of traditional religious structures started to fade, and this helped to cause the popularity of spiritualism. The belief that mediums can talk to the dead and channel the dead was part of the core of spiritualism.

Harry Houdini set up many different seances with many different spiritual mediums in order to contact his mother. Interestingly enough, Harry Houdini himself actually set up fake seances in his own career in show business. As such, he was particularly qualified to recognize many of the fake seances that he encountered for what they were. In this case, the false nature of these sessions truly must have been difficult to watch for Harry Houdini, given what he was trying to accomplish.

Harry Houdini as a Ghost Hunter

However, the frustrations that he encountered as a grieving man who was just looking for answers probably motivated him to become a much more successful ghost hunter and debunking expert. Soon, debunking the fake mediums started to become the entire purpose of Harry Houdini's endeavors, and this led to a situation where he was almost trying to get revenge on the people who seemed to take advantage of other grieving individuals.

Many people today who are motivated by debunking different claims are going to strongly criticize the people who seek out mediums. They will come at the issue from a position of superiority. However, Harry Houdini was someone who really wanted to contact his mother, and this was in spite of the fact that he had already built up a lot of experience with mysticism and the world of spiritualism. Harry Houdini lambasted the false spiritualist mediums for the ways in which they exploited people, and there seemed to be part of him that wanted to get back at them.

Many ghost hunters have had motivations of that variety as well. There are ghost hunters who are true believers and there are ghost hunters who are actually just interested in testing the claims. One way or another, these people are going to be interested in actually getting to the bottom of the different claims.

Harry Houdini's Mission

One of the interesting things about Harry Houdini is that he was not approaching the issue in the manner of a modern skeptic. He was interested in debunking mystical claims, but this was partly in an effort to find the real thing. He still wanted to be able to contact the dead and he wanted the dead to have the ability to contact the living. While lots of modern skeptics keep on trying to debunk these claims in the manner of scientists disproving hypotheses, Harry Houdini was more like a believer who wanted to find the right source of faith.

Harry Houdini actually told his friends that he would try to contact them after he died if such a thing were possible, which is an interesting thing to imagine. He actually established a code with his wife Bess, so that if Bess was contacted by a spirit in the event of Harry Houdini's death, it would be possible to identify the spirit as him in the first place.

Bess lived up to her word and she became something of a ghost hunter herself when Harry Houdini died, as luck would have it, on Halloween. She used many of the methods that he had taught her and that she had learned from a lifetime of watching him. She tried to manipulate the environment around her, letting certain atmospheres and circumstances unfold in the hope that this would let Harry Houdini's spirit actually find her.

Many ghost hunters do the same thing today. They try to create emotional associations in the hope that spirits are going to find their way back, partly operating under the idea that spirits are lost and that spirits are going to need something that is going to bind them to the world. Spirits are thought to be highly emotional, since they no longer have bodies and everything about them is just sensation. Manipulating the emotional climate of an area is thought to draw the spirits.

Some of the terms associated with ghost hunting from this time period, such as ectoplasm, are still in use today. Many ghost hunters use the methods that Bess and Harry Houdini used in order to contact members of their own family. People look for strange sounds and they try to pinpoint the locations of ghosts, while also attempting to draw them out somewhat. Today, conducting séances is less common. Hunting for ghosts is much more physical and involves more legwork these days. However, the intent is still there, and a lot of people are still going to be looking for ghosts with the same vision and motivation as the Houdini family.

CHAPTER THREE
ARTHUR CONAN DOYLE

Arthur Conan Doyle, though, was a physician by his professional and formal qualifications, although he is not nearly as well-known as a physician than as a novelist. His works related to the genre of the detective solving mystery gained him fame in the 19th and 20th century. His works, still to this day, are known worldwide. Sherlock Holmes, now in major films and a TV series is still praised, as the author who is delicately remembered and honored for his work.

Though we know so much about Sherlock Holmes, the movie and the TV series, the creator of the character himself, he is someone we may not know much about. So, who was Sir Arthur Conan Doyle? That is going to be briefly explained in the text below.

Early Age:

Arthur Conan Doyle was born in Edinburgh, Scotland on 22nd May 1859. His father, Charles A. Doyle was a painter of the Victorian times and was of Irish descent. His mother held the same descent. The two married in 1855 and Arthur had 2 siblings, Connie Doyle and Innes Doyle. Arthur attended his basic school in Lancashire from 1868 to 1870. He would then attend Stonyhurst College and later advance his education in Austria.

Career as a physician:

He would study medicine in Edinburgh in 1876 and work in Aston (which is now a part of Birmingham). Doyle studied practical Botany there and would complete his studies in 1881. He completed his Doctor of medicine degree in 1885 on the subject of an infectious disease which would render the spine present in lower back useless and therefore let the person not attain a fixed position.

His career as a medical professional didn't seem to go quite well, although his initial academic publication did earn him quite a reputation in murder investigations that are held in the 21st century. As far as his career went, that didn't go well as the professional bond between him and his classmate wouldn't advance. Started on his own in South sea, he was unable to attract patients or hold patients to pursue his career. It was during this period of his life where he'd write and thus giving birth to the famous Sherlock Holmes and many of his other masterpieces.

Literature:

Sir Arthur Conan Doyle, though may have been a physician in his professional and formal life, he was never able to become the famous physician that as he'd expected himself to be. It was perhaps this phase which made him realize that he was better off being a literary man than a medical one.

• Sherlock Holmes:

Sherlock Holmes was a fictional character who'd solve crime mysteries that were way beyond the intelligence of ordinary people. He was portrayed a composed, logical, and a firm man. Arthur's first literary work would introduce the famous fictional character Sherlock Holmes and his partner Dr. Watson in 1887. The series of Sherlock Holmes and his adventures would last up to 4 novels while the final was published in 1914. Sherlock Holmes would also appear in numerous short stories that were composed by Arthur himself. A total of 56 short stories were based on Sherlock Holmes.

• Professor Challenger:

Professor Challenger would become one of the literary works of Arthur Conan Doyle. The first time he'd appear in publication was in 1912. This was around the time when Sherlock was about to have the final novel on him. Unlike anything that Sherlock was, Challenger was the total opposite and he was written to be a hot-headed, scientific, and a man of domination. Professor Challenger would have 2 novels, 1 novella and 1 short story on him.

Beliefs:

Arthur Conan Doyle left Christianity to become an agnostic and later became a spiritualist.

Death:

Arthur Conan Doyle died in 1930 at the age of 71 due to a cardiac arrest. His last words were to his wife in which he said she is wonderful. Arthur rests in New Forest, Hampshire, along with his wife.

Legacy:

Sir Arthur Conan Doyle is known to be one of the most famous fictional writers of his times. He not only introduced and immortalized Sherlock Holmes, but he also paved way for detective writings which would form a whole new genre of thrillers, crime, mystery and detective fiction. Wherever

Sherlock Holmes will be mentioned, the name Arthur Conan Doyle will always be associated with it.

CHAPTER FOUR
MINA MARGERY CRANDON

Mina "Margery" Crandon, (aka Margery the Medium) became famous for being a physical medium during the turn of the century. She grew up on a farm in Princeton, Ontario, Canada. Although, she did end up moving to the city of Boston.

Since her admittance of being able to talk to the dead, notably the 'channeling' of her dead brother, Walter Stinson, she was widely discredited because of it. In other words, many didn't believe her. The fact that she channeled-in the non-living with those that were living was not really a good trait for women in those days.

During a time when women were struggling for equality, it didn't hold well in the society she was living in. She ended up falling in love and married a grocer, Earl Rand, while she was a secretary for her local church. They had a son together soon after they got married.

Although, later she sued for divorce from Mr. Rand.

Months later, she got married again with the surgeon she met at a hospital. She fell in love with the doctor who did surgery on her at a Dorchester, Massachusetts hospital; it was rumored that she had appendicitis.

Months later she 'bumped into him' again while they were working in a hospital in New England during the first World War. She was a volunteer ambulance driver and he was a surgeon at the Naval Hospital. Soon she was married to this man, Dr. Le Roi Goddard Cranton. He ended up adopting her son; Mina eventually change his name to John Crandon.

Dr. Crandon was a wealthy surgeon. She moved into his home on 10 Lime Street on Beacon Hill in Boston.

Although, the majority of people they frequented didn't obliged to 'medium work.' Yet, it also gave her a rather peculiar demeanor in character according to the high society her husband Dr. Cranton socialized with, she seemed to not mind. Plus, since she was the wife of a wealthy surgeon and socialite, why should they.

As Margary the Medium

On the other hand, some people were entertained by her special "gift" eventually.

Although it was her 'charm and lack of interest in personal monetary rewards' that made her more honest to in the public eye. She was also credible to Sir Arthur Conan Doyle, one of her most famous supporters. There were also others: some luminary members of the upper class in Boston which included some Ivy League elite.

The challenge; the real medium work

When Mina started utilizing her 'so called gift of medium work' in seances,' she did it as a hobby. Everything became discredited by Houdini the magician and others in the scientific society. Since many, especially, Houdini, felt she cheated many in her quest to be para-normally gifted, she would of won the reward that was supposed to be given by the demonstrating her telekinetic abilities to the Scientific American Magazine and scientists and doctors. Yet, she failed when they tied her up to prove she had no paranormal abilities. This was proven more than once.

It was said that the magician Houdini didn't want her to be the one to win. Yet he didn't have to prove anything, because she eventually ended up be found a fraud later on in her.

She demonstrated her work as a medium through special occasions and through public events. Obviously, her claim to her medium works didn't hold well with the magician Houdini, nor with the overall public.

Sources: https://www.bing.com/search?q=Mina+Crandon+&form=PRUSEN&mkt=en-us&httpsmsn=1&refig=11ddbf81c58546a094859febc3ac020b&sp=-1&pq=mina+crandon+&sc=8-13&qs=n&sk=&cvid=11ddbf81c58546a094859febc3ac020b

http://www.historynet.com/mina-crandon-harry-houdini-the-medium-
and-the-magician.htm

CHAPTER FIVE ARTHUR FORD

If you needed a way to contact the famed magician and spiritualist, Harry Houdini, and his mother, who would you call? Probably not Ghost-busters. Instead, until about 40 years ago, you might have called a famous psychic and medium named Arthur Ford.

To at least a great extent, Arthur Ford set the stage for many of what we today call television spiritual hucksters such as Sylvia Browne, John Edward. James van Praagh, and others who make scandalous amounts of money playing on the susceptibility of the gullible and the bereaved.

Born in 1896, Ford started his spiritual path when he took a religious pilgrimage during which he explored several Protestant denominations: Episcopalian-ism to the Baptists to Unitarianism and finally ending at Transylvania College, a small Disciples of Christ college in Kentucky. He enrolled, resulting in a degree and eventually his ordination as a Disciples minister. He served for a short time at a church in Kentucky before the outbreak of World War I, when he enlisted. It was during this service that he discovered his psychic abilities, claiming he "heard" the names of soldiers several days before they appeared on casualty lists.

Ford and the Spiritualist Movement

Around 1921, after a period of investigating psychic phenomenon, Ford found himself a part of the growing spiritualist movement of the era. Eventually settling in New York City and serving as the minister of a spiritualist church. It was during this time that he emerged from a trance session with a spirit guide he referred to as "Fletcher," who he claimed controlled him for the remainder of his life.

Ford, by this time, was becoming wildly popular, giving lectures both in the United States and abroad. During one of these sessions, the veteran Spiritualist and author Sir Arthur Conan Doyle attended and later referred to Ford as "One of the most amazing things I have ever seen in 41 years of psychic experience." It was shortly after this that the widow of famed magician and illusionist Harry Houdini, Bess, attended one of Ford's lectures, with Doyle's encouragement.

The Houdini Hoax

It was also with Doyle's encouragement that Bess Houdini started believing that Ford could contact the spirit of her husband, Harry, who had died on Halloween in 1926. In 1928, Ford made the claim that he, with the help of his spirit guide, "Fletcher," was able to reach Houdini's mother, and about a year later, the famed magician himself. Ford did this using the "proof" of relaying the full text of a secret message that Harry had given his wife for this purpose of authentication.

Initially, Bess supported Ford's claims, but since that time several authors have suggested that her endorsement of his claims might have been due in part to the effects of alcoholism as well as a crush she might have had on him. Further, other researchers have suggested that Ford's own situation might have also contributed to the issue since after an auto accident he was involved in caused a severe Morphine addiction he suffered with until his death as well as alcoholism that he suffered with until shortly before his death.

Bess Houdini later repudiated her endorsement of Ford's claims, adding to that the skepticism reported by several experts, including Milbourne Christopher, a magician, illusionist, and author who spent many of his years debunking the work of psychics who claimed powers to be actually using magic trickery.

Even in Ford's lifetime, there were skeptics who pointed out that Ford may have had help learning the code not only from popular media reporting that he could have easily seen, but several reporters even claimed that they were told by Ford himself that Bess Houdini had given him the code. Ford later rebuked these claims as the work of an "impostor."

After Ford's death in 1971, Allen Spraggett, author of Arthur Ford, The Man who Talked with the Dead, along with a collaborator, Rev. William V. Rauscher uncovered significant evidence leading to the conclusion that the contact Ford had claimed with Harry Houdini and his mother had, indeed, be faked. Further, it was revealed that Ford had access to several sources that revealed the Houdini code. Among these were a book titled Houdini: His Life Story, which detailed the code on page 105, as well as in Ford's own files, which included a collection of newspaper clippings, obituaries, and other information disguised as bound poetry books, which researchers claim enabled Ford to research his clients' backgrounds.

The Bishop Pike Controversy

In 1967 Ford again emerged to prominence during a television interview centering on the subject of life after death, when he put himself into a trance and delivered several messages to Episcopal bishop James Pike, from his son, who had committed suicide the previous year. One message claimed to be from Pike's son and another from another prominent theologian Paul Tillich. Impressed, Pike later affirmed his belief in the reality of psychic phenomena in his book, The Other Side. The television program also served to revive public interest in Spiritualism and psychic phenomena. Within a month Ford received more than 12,000 letters as a result. It was only after Ford's death that Allen Spraggett and William Rauscher, while compiling materials for his biography, discovered his notes for the session among his papers, revealing the fact that he faked the famous seance.

Death and Beyond

After Ford's death in Miami in 1971, not only did researchers find still more evidence of Ford's frauds, but one author, Ruth Montgomery, claimed to have received psychic messages from Ford, all of which she included in her book, A World Beyond. No matter where a person might stand on the subject of Ford and his claims, there is little doubt that the bulk of his fame rests on the credibility of the Houdini code, which is subject to considerable controversy, regardless of which position you want to side with. Regardless, the debate will probably continue as long as the subject elicits interest in those who want to discuss it.

CHAPTER SIX
ARTHUR CONAN DOYLE
SPIRITUALIST

Sir Arthur Conan Doyle is famously known as the author to the Sherlock Holmes books, and even though his character, Sherlock Holmes, was infused with skepticism and rationalism, Doyle was not. There are not many who know what Sir Arthur Doyle did outside of writing his famous Sherlock Holmes stories, and it is not a well-known fact that he fell in love with the paranormal world, and decided to jump into it and become involved within this field. In 1866, he became incredibly interested in the field of the paranormal, and he became involved within the realm of Spiritualism. Sir Arthur found inspiration from several different individuals who were involved in the spiritual and paranormal field at this time, and his interest in this area, led him to seek out his own spiritual experiences. After he jumped into the world of supernatural and paranormal happenings, he took off with his beliefs and became a big part of investigating anything that he could in the paranormal.

The Beginning

Once Sir Arthur Doyle took the first steps into investigating the paranormal, he called upon a teacher at Greenwich Naval Academy, General Drayson, and he had him participate in the art of table turning during a paranormal investigation, and then had him convinced of telepathy as well. Doyle became very interested in the paranormal by this point, and had dove into the field even deeper.

In 1893, the British Society of Psychical Research was founded, and Conan Doyle was one of the very first members that became a part of this society for the paranormal. There were several other individuals who joined in this society as well, and many of them were scientists, or worked in the field of science. This was the time and age, when spiritualism had not yet been defined as either religion, or as science. So, to confirm the claims of the several different spiritualists, this organization conducted several different experiments to try and confirm the existence of paranormal phenomenon. This led Doyle to come to the conclusion that telepathy, or thought transference as he called it, was a real phenomenon that did in fact exist, and he was very excited to continue on down the path of experimenting in the paranormal.

Arthur's Journey Through The Paranormal

Doyle became so involved with his new found interest, that he began giving lectures on spiritualism all around the world. He went to major cities in New

Zealand, Australia, and even in England, and while he was in England, he met Harry Houdini who was on his own adventure in England with his magic shows. Houdini had become an idol of Conan Doyle, and he had admired this magician for many years, and even though Houdini did not have at the time have an interest in spiritualism or seances, he and Doyle became very good friends right from the start. However, after Houdini accompanied Sir Arthur in a seance with Jean Doyle, who claimed to have contacted Houdini's mother and wrote everything in English,(his mother neither read or wrote in English) Houdini labeled them as frauds and ended his friendship with them.

Doyle then went on to publish a book about the existence of fairies, and it came from photographs that two young girls had claimed to have taken of real fairies. However, there were several who questioned Doyle's sanity when these photos were said to be fraudulent as well, but Arthur Doyle kept trying to convince the world that this was not a fraud.

In the 1920's, he spent time in the United States and led several different lectures on spiritualism and the paranormal. Then his journey led him to South Africa, and then to the European countries where he was named as the honorary president of the first International Spiritualism Congress that resided in Paris, France.

The Ending Of His Journey

As Sir Arthur Conan Doyle came to the ending of his life, he said that he wanted to be remembered as a spiritualist more so that as an author. He was able to obtain this title, (spiritualist) right after his death. There are several who said that Arthur and his wife, had worked out a specific type of system in which they could communicate to each other after one of them had passed on. So, just five days after Doyle had passed away, there was a seance that was held for him to be able to communicate with his wife Jean Doyle. As the seance began, the medium, who was performing the seance, claimed that she could see Arthur Doyle sitting in an empty chair and that he had a message for his wife Jean. Then as the medium began to relay this message to her, she was drowned out by organ music and no one, but Jean, knows what the message was that Arthur wanted Jean to know.

Conclusion

In conclusion, Sir Arthur Conan Doyle wanted to be well-known for his spiritualism, unfortunately for him his books and short stories were so immensely popular that they buried for almost a century this important part of his life. It is funny how life does that to most of us whether we live small private lives or lives in the bright glare of the public it will be others who record our history. It will be up to others to backtrack through our lives and to determine from our efforts what was truly important to each and every one of us. Sir Arthur Conan Doyle created an amazing character that has entertained million and has made this character's views on deductive reasoning the basis for criminal investigations around the world. The fact that has been almost forgotten is that this same approach to solving crimes has been used for decades by those who investigate the paranormal.

Every paranormal investigator owes a debt of gratitude to this man and his remarkable life.

Sir Arthur Conan Doyle, author, spiritualist and paranormal investigator.

PARANORMAL INVESTIGATORS BOOK 9

MONTAGUE SUMMERS
TELL ME STRANGE THINGS

By.

Rodney C. Cannon

CHAPTER THE WRITINGS OF MONTAGUE SUMMERS

- All magic, all witchcraft, depends on the Devil, and is fundamentally evil. - MONTAGUE SUMMERS,

Montague Summers and Aleister Crowley had a rather odd friendship. Although he was against it, Summers' primary interest was with the occult. Summers and Crowley were quite close and would have frequent meetings discussing their bond and friendship. In his book The History of Witchcraft and Demonology, Summers is writing about a witch, claiming that she is "a minister to vice and inconceivable corruption." This was the first piece of work that Summers was recognized for, written to educate people during that time and to teach the traits and history of witchcraft. It's obvious that Summers was against witchcraft and believed strongly in the word of God, but in his English translation of Malleus Maleficarum, he also insisted that real witchcraft was a part of Catholic doctrine.

Summers began to look for a different angle and started to become fascinated with vampires and werewolves. He began by writing a book titled The Vampire: His Kith and Kin In 1928. In this book, Summers addresses his belief in vampires, claiming that they are just as real as birds. His beliefs not only in vampires escalated, and he wrote another book later titled The Vampire in Europe In 1929. In this text, Summers mentions very real possibilities and occurrences of vampires found throughout Europe. His first chapter discusses instances of vampires in Ancient Greece and Rome.

This work, while sounding a bit made up, is actually put together by research, and contains footnotes and quotes, showing the so called " evidence" Summers used when comprising this piece of literature. In 1933, Summers wrote a book titled The Werewolf, in which he discussed the subjects of shapeshifting, the difference between werewolves and lycanthropy, which is the ability for a person to transform into an animal. He believed that the works of witches, vampires, and werewolves were the work of the devil, and tried to educate those who knew very little about these topics.

While it was known that Summers and Crowley were friends, Crowley also had his fair share of written work pertaining to his beliefs. His first and most known piece is titled The Book of The Law or Liber AL vel Liges. In this work, Crowley wrote about a "new stage" of humanity coming. This story and origin of the book had begun in the early 1900s when Summers had performed the "Bornless Ritual" on his wife, causing her to repeat the phrase, "They're waiting for you." She had stated the person waiting for Crowley was "Horus," which led him to ask her multiple questions about what she saw, such as its appearance and meaning behind it.

Crowley had also written a book titled The Equinox of The Gods, in which he wrote about the encounter with Horus in more detail, and was the first book which detailed the events he went through leading up to The Book of The Law. Along with this story, there are also personal diary entries from Crowley, allowing the reader to get a better look in detail of the events that took place. Both works of these authors, despite their many opposing beliefs, reflected their opinions and showed how much work they truly put into getting their thoughts out to the public.

CHAPTER TWO THE MALLEUS MALEFICARUM

MALLEVS
MALEFICARVM,
MALEFICAS ET EARVM
haeresim frameâ conterens,

EX VARIIS AVCTORIBVS COMPILATVS,
& in quatuor Tomos iustè distributus,

QVORVM DVO PRIORES VANAS DÆMONVM
versutias, praestigiosas eorum delusiones, superstitiosas Strigimagarum
caeremonias, horrendos etiam cum illis congressus; exactam denique
tam pestifera sectae disquisitionem, & punitionem complectuntur.
Tertius praxim Exorcistarum ad Dæmonum, & Strigimagarum male-
ficia de Christi fidelibus pellenda; Quartus verò Artem Doctrinalem,
Benedictionalem, & Exorcismalem continent.

TOMVS PRIMVS.
Indices Auctorum, capitum, rerùmque non desunt,

Editio novissima, infinitis penè mendis expurgata; cuique accessit Fuga
Dæmonum & Complementum artis exorcisticae.

Vir sive mulier, in quibus Pythonicus, vel divinationis fuerit spiritus, morte moriatur;
Levitici cap. 10.

LVGDVNI,
Sumptibus CLAVDII BOVRGEAT, sub signo Mercurij Galli.

M. DC. LXIX.
CVM PRIVILEGIO REGIS

The Malleus Maleficarum, which is translated to Hammer of Witches, is a trea-
tise on witchcraft written in Latin and first published in the year 1487. Com-

piled by Dominican inquisitors Heinrich Kramer and Jacob Sprenger, the trea-
tise argues for the extinction of witches and develops detailed legal and theological theories on why it endorses this. A surprising fact about this book is
that it was once extremely popular, a bestseller even, and was second only to the
Bible in terms of sales for almost 200 years. Its popularity was spread outside of
Germany, and the book had a huge influence in Spain, Italy, and England.

The Malleus Maleficarum equates sorcery or witchcraft to heresy, one of
the worst crimes one could commit during those times, and provides grimly detailed practices for inquisitors on how to recognize those practicing witchcraft.
It became a guidebook for inquisitors to use at the time, and had a huge impact
on their behavior towards the accused.

During this medieval period in history, it was common practice to torture
heretics, and The Malleus Maleficarum suggests that the same should be done
to witches for the purpose of making them confess to their crimes. It suggests
that the death penalty (which often meant being burnt at the stake), was the
only effective method of ridding the world of witchcraft.

The Malleus Maleficarum had a notable effect on witch trials and the torture involved during them and continued to influence the increasingly brutal
persecution of those claimed to be witches. During the time of its publication,
there were many vocal figures within the Christian community to dispelled the
claims that witchcraft was real, or that real witches existed, and claimed it was
mere superstition going too far. The Malleus Maleficarum silenced those voices
by ultimately equating witchcraft with heresy, and announcing witchcraft as a
threat not just to society, but to the Christian world as a whole. This scared people into even suggesting heretic behavior by denouncing the existence of witches, so people became scared to voice their opinions about witchcraft in fear of
themselves being put on trial.

The book is a collection of various stories featuring witchcraft, hearsay, confessions, and accusations that are to be regarded as supposed "evidence" that the
existence of witches is a real and approaching threat. There is barely any original
material by Kramer and Sprenger in The Malleus Maleficarum, just resources
which they have compiled.

Accusations during the time could be made by anyone, and once that accu-
sation was heard it wasn't long before the accused was put to trial regardless of
any physical evidence of committing the crime. It was particularly worrying for

women who were herb gatherers, midwives, widows, and spinsters - those without men in their lives suffered the worst fear of being accused because of this generated suspicion amongst people.

The book is divided into three parts. Each section raises particular concerns and provides arguments against them and methods for dealing with them.

Part one provides a detailed speculation about the existence of witchcraft and seeks to prove it real. Here, the authors suggest that witches are followers of the Devil, who carry out this following through evil behavior. It suggests that women, as the inferior sex, are by nature more prone to the lure of the Devil. The book declares that the word for woman, Femina, derives from the words fe+minus, meaning faithless. This declaration is, however, incorrect.

Part two deals with different forms of witchcraft and what they entail. The existence of the Devil and witches as his followers are dealt with as facts in The Malleus Maleficarum. Heinrich and Sprenger suggest ways in which victims can reverse the effects of spells cast by witches, and details what these spells might be and what purpose they serve. Many of the facts presented in the book are taken from "confessions" obtained during the author's' inquisitorial practices, therefore the truth in them is questionable.

The third part provides a report of the methods inquisitors should undertake when trying supposed witches, as well as how to detect whether or not they are lying, and how to the problem should be dealt with once it is confirmed. Torture is the only option if the witch hasn't confessed willingly. They suggest that hearsay within the public is sufficient evidence that a woman ought to be tried for being a witch. Helpfully, they do suggest that accusations should be investigated properly in order to separate truth from malicious intent. Additionally, they state that if the defense of the witch is too successful or intense, that it must be that the witch has put a spell on them. Therefore, according to the book the woman on trial was mostly doomed from the very beginning. They provide a set of rules which should be followed to prevent authorities from bewitchment, and of course, the inquisitors are already working in God's name, so they can't possibly be at risk of having a spell cast on them.

Overall, the book manifests the mentality of the middle ages, as it constantly presses on the idea of women as the inferior species both physically and intellectually. Behaviour such as animal transformations, flight, changing the weather and much more are attributed to witchcraft and were carried out in the name of the Devil. The book is written in a tone which is completely flat and realistic, which shows that the writers were completely serious in all the information that they were trying to convey as truth. The book has had a huge impact on how witchcraft was dealt with, and how witches were tried and introduced many new methods for detecting and destroying a witch. Despite it being contested by many during the time, the book managed to convey its ideas as factual, therefore enlisting people to believe that they were writing in the name of protecting the world of God from the evils of the Devil, evils which were carried out by witches. The book is obviously problematic when looked back on now, considering that it caused the deaths of a lot of women during the time due to its basis in "factual information". But, during the time, people were easily convinced that the ideas in the book were real and pointed to a real threat to humanity.

CHAPTER THREE HEINRICH KRAMER

Heinrich Kramer, also known as Henricus Institor, just might be considered the "grandfather" of witchcraft extermination. It's somewhat hard to believe that the person who may have actually inspired the Salem Witch Trials was not from anywhere near Salem, nor even the United States. With that being said, he definitely got the ball rolling when it came to things of that nature, even though he did so half a world away and during a much earlier time.

Born Heinrich Kramer, he was ultimately given his Latinized name, Henricus Institor, because of his work through the Church. Kramer lived from approximately 1430 to 1505. Although his date of death is certain, his birth date is not quite as firm. However, it was a common practice during that time for people that were highly involved in the Church to have Latinized names as well as birth names. Although this might be considered something of a distinguishing trait, this is certainly not what he is best known for.

Kramer was of German descent and was heavily involved in the Catholic Church. As was a rather common practice at the time, he was considered not only a Churchman but also an inquisitor. In other words, it was his job to seek out those responsible of heresy in the eyes of the Church and then call them out.

He took this job very seriously and ultimately, he even wrote a number of books on the subject. One such book was titled "Malleus Maleficarum," a book he wrote in 1487 on witchcraft. It is important to remember that this book was not written with the intention of merely educating people about the subject of witchcraft, nor even how to recognize and avoid it.

Instead, this book was written for the express purpose of teaching people how to recognize not only witchcraft, but witches, and to exterminate them. His goal was to get rid of every witch he or anyone else could find, as being a witch was viewed as extreme heresy within the eyes of the Church. This book was essentially what started the witch trials that occurred during the early modern period. More importantly, the book could be used as the basis for further witch trials that occurred later on.

Today, some people might consider Kramer's views extreme. However, many would readily agree that the Church still holds many of the same views that were written about in this book so many years ago. The truth is, there is still a great deal of debate concerning the subject of witchcraft. Many of those who participate in its claim that they are only good witches who do no harm to anyone, but the Church sees things quite differently. Perhaps they are not targeting the individuals these days so much as they are targeting the idea of practicing witchcraft.

Most people, with the exception of those who choose to practice it, would likely agree that even when an individual thinks they are a "good" witch, there is a problem because they are essentially praying to and worshipping something other than Jesus Christ. In addition, there is always the chance that they will inadvertently invite something very dark into their lives, and by default, into the lives of all those around them, largely because they are not giving control to God. This is a long-standing issue within the Church and is not likely to go away anytime in the near future.

Back when Kramer was alive, the rules regarding heresy within the Church were indeed much more stringent. Although things have relaxed somewhat in the present day, the Church itself still feels much the same way as it did back then. For obvious reasons, that is not likely to change. While the Church may not employ people like Kramer any longer, there is still a very big divide between the two sides. This essentially means that people have to decide which camp they are going to fall into and then keep in line.

Even in popular culture, witchcraft is a common subject. It's interesting to note that the resulting witch trials really do have their roots in history. It lends some credence to a subject that is otherwise often thought of as nothing more than a Halloween prank.

Source: Jolly, Raudvere, & Peters(eds.), "Witchcraft and magic in Europe: the Middle Ages", page 241 (2002)

CHAPTER FOUR ALEISTER CROWLEY

Aleister Crowley was born in October 1875 and had a mind ahead of his time. He was an occultist, poet, magician, painter, and mountaineer. He was also the founder of the Thelema religion and considered himself to be a prophet. He felt that he was granted the power to guide his fellow humans and lead them to the Eon of Horus in the early part of the 20th century. Due to his great writing abilities, his works reached thousands of people all over the world and his religious views were widely published.

Crowley was born into wealth in Warwickshire, England. His family was religious but he did not share in their ideas or beliefs in the Christian faith. He was interested in studying Western esotericism. After high school, Crowley continued his studies at the University of Cambridge. He focused on poetry and had several of his works published. Some researchers suggest that at this time he was recruited as a spy for the British Intelligence Agency. It was suggested that he continued to work as a spy for the rest of his life.

In 1989 Crowley began to look for a higher meaning and got involved in mystical adventures. He joined the Hermit Order of the Golden Dawn where he studied and was trained to perform ceremonial magic. After completing his training Crowley moved outside of lake Loch Ness in Scotland. He worked with Oscar Eckenstein and they studied Buddhism practices. While studied he fell in love with Rose Edith Kelly and they married. While the couple was on their honeymoon in Egypt Crowley is said to have had a supernatural experience. He stated that a supernatural entity called Aiwass came to his. Aiwass was said to have given him The Book of Law which was the text behind his Thelema religion. After this experience, he stated that people should align themselves with their true will. In order to get in touch with this true will, a person had to follow the teachings of magick.

In 1907 Crowley began his religious writings. He still performed Abramelin rituals. At this time he stated that he reached the statehood of Samadhi where he became a union with a God like figure. When he was writing the Holy Books of Thelma is was stated that Crowley was using hashish heavily especially during his rituals. He continued to write the Holy Books of Thelma based on what he said Aiwass was dictating to him.

While Crowley was writing his holy books he needed a way to earn money. While he was writing these religious books he was working for George Montagu Bennett who was the Earl of Tankerville. Crowley's job was to help protect the Earl from witchcraft. Crowley provided this service but did not think that the Earl was really haunted. It turned out the Earl had an addiction to cocaine that made him paranoid. Crowley began teaching others magical practice, however. He taught a group of students how to perform some of this magic as well as instructed them in the occult. Crowley began a sexual relationship with one of his students named Victor Nueburg. This relationship was very risky. Not only was Crowley married with children but homosexual relationships were taboo at this time. While all of this was going on Crowley continued to write his books. He wrote Liber 777 which was a book of magic. He also tried to write some short horror stories.

The year 1907 continued to be busy for Crowley. He formed a cult to become the leader of the Hermetic Order of the Golden Dawn. He had several others to aid him and they also held high ranking positions. By 1909 Crowley did something else that was unheard of at this time. He got a divorce from his wife. He claimed that she had a problem with alcohol. They continued to be close and even stayed living in the same household. By 1911 Rose became so caught up in her addiction that she had to be institutionalized.

The problems at home did not stop Crowley from traveling the world. He traveled to Algeria and went about the Middle East reading passages from the Quran. He also got in touch with Enochian magic at this time. Crowley studied some unusual types of magic as well. He discovered a sex magic ritual as well as ways to invoke demonic spirits and blood sacrifices. While one cannot say if he was really able to evoke a spirit it did make Crowley famous. He enjoyed the same and even played up human sacrifices and Satanic rituals even though he did not practice either. What he did like about this image was the newfound fame that came along with it.

The fame brought additional follows to listen to the words of Aleister Crowley. In order to reach even more people, he developed the Rites of Artemis which was a performance featuring both magical acts as well as symbolism with the members. For the most part, the reviews on these performances were positive. Even when there was a negative review it did not bother Crowley. He did lose some of his trusted members due to the negative reviews and allegations of

homosexual activity. Crowley did continue to write additional religious material and even changed the spelling of magic to magick. The new spelling of magick was said to represent paranormal phenomenon that was at work. This new
word also sounded like a great addition to this stage act.

In the year 1912 Crowley published what became to be known as his
most well-received book. It was also considered to be his greatest success. He
was accused of publishing secrets of the club. Crowley took his love of magic
and mixed it with sexual practices. Crowley took his magical practices and increased his interest in sex magic. He had several practices that involved anal sex
and many members participated in this magical practice. As part of many of the
magic rituals, couples were asked to perform sex acts as part of the magic. Other
couples were often involved in this practice. Crowley was highly criticized for
mixing both magic and adverse sexual practices.

Aleister Crowley made his living off of donations from group members and
the membership dues that people had to pay to be part of his cult. When the
first World War broke out he was living in New York City in the United States.
He began to write for the magazine Vanity Fair while he continued with his
experiments that involve sex magic. This magic involved masturbation, prosti-
tution, and males that had homosexual experiences with others. Crowley supported Germany during this war and joined in the pro-German protests. During this time it was said that he was working as a double agent. He was said to
be a spy for Britain while supporting the German Army.

Crowley continued to protest Britain during the war. In 1916 he went on
a magic retreat in Lake Pasquancey with his new love interest. At this time he

used drugs heavily and took part in a ritual where he named himself Master Therion. At this time he also wrote several short stories. By 1918 he went on another religious retreat where he translated the Tae Te Ching and used the teachings that he liked in his own religion. With the help of his supporters, he was able to write and public The Equinox and several other volumes that went along with this text.

By 1920 Crowley went back to live in London. He was called scum for helping the Germans during the war. He developed asthma and was given heroin by a doctor. He quickly became addicted to this and did not even know it. He moved to Paris to escape this and had new and exciting sexual experiences. This added to these religion teachings including the ménage a trios.

By 1923 many people considered Crowley to be an evil man and did not approve of his practices. Crowley was asked to leave several European countries including Italy. He settled in the city of Berlin in 1930. He ended up back in London and since he needed the money he filed lawsuits against people he claimed lied about him in public. He lost the case and finally had to file for bankruptcy. For a number of years, he had been spending more money than he was making. Upon his return to Germany, Crowley was intrigued by Adolf Hitler. He thought he would be able to convert Hitler to his Thelema religion. Hitler showed no interested and imprisoned someone that Crowley was close to. From that point on Crowley thought of Hitler as a black magician and had nothing to do with him.

When World War II broke out Crowley offered his services to the Naval Intelligence Division but they were not interested in his services. Britain rejected any help that he was willing to offer them. Both his asthma and his addiction to heroin got worse during this time. During one of his hospital stays Crowley developed his own set of tarot card with his own designs. He even wrote a book called Liber Oz in his own attempt to end the war. As his end neared he continued to write and even wrote the book Magick Without Tears.

Crowley knew that his end was near. He started appointing his followers to higher positions and passed his teachings onto them. He worked with others that were in the world of magick and even contributed to books that they were writing. He kept himself surrounded by family and others that were close to him. Crowley died on December 1st in 1947 from chronic bronchitis and pleurisy. These conditions were set off due to old age. At the time of his death,

Crowley was 72 years old. At this funeral teachings from some of his books were read. The press called his funeral the Black Mass.

Crowley's Thelma religion was described as a new religious movement. Others called it a form of modern Paganism. Thelema took shape after The Book of Modern Law was published. In his autobiography, Crowley stated that his life was to be the oriental wisdom to Europe and to bring paganism to a pure form. His religion was influenced not only by teachings of the occult buy by beliefs in Hinduism, Buddhism, naturalism, magic, astrology, tarot, and other influences. He also took influences from yoga and tantra to add to his beliefs. During the 20th century, he thought that humans would take on the Aoen which is a belief in their destiny. He thought that each person had their own true will and should discover their own path to pursue it. He even referred to it as the Great Work. He chose to use magick spells to help get to a higher personal level. He thought this was a form of self-expression and believed that magic would lead to new advances in science. He felt that practicing magick would help a person adapt to the changes and advances in the scientific community. Sex was a big part of his religion and thought that it could be used for personal expression. Sex was a sacrament and sexual fluids, as well as menstrual blood, were a big part of his ceremonies. These fluids were considered to be Cakes of Light.

Aleister Crowley was considered to be a very influential person and stood out from other during this time. He was not afraid to express his belief in ghost, vampire, the occult, and other religious practices. Some people said he was a genius while others thought he was cruel. He was not afraid to do things that made him stand out and was willing to revolt against anything that was popular or moral at the time. He lived until the month of December in 1947. During this life, he was able to influence a large number of people and did not back away if something was not popular. Crowley stood up for his own belief even if they were considered to be odd and eccentric.

CHAPTER FIVE AUGUSTUS MONTAGUE SUMMERS

Augustus Montague Summers also known by just Montague Summers was an author as well as a clergyman from England. He is known for his work during the 17th century and some of his studies. He was one of the first people at this time to study witches, vampires, and werewolves. He believed in the existence of all of those creatures. He was also the first person to translate the witch hunter's manual from the 15th century into English so that more people could read and understand it.

Simmers was born in 1880 and he was the youngest of a family with five children. He studied theology at Trinity College in Oxford and his intentions were to become a priest in the Church of England. In 1905 he did get a college degree and decided to continue his studies focusing on religion at the Lichfield Theology College. In 1908 Summers became a deacon and worked in the Greater Bristol area. At this time there were some rumors that he was interested in Satanism and there were also rumors that he was involved in sexual relationships with young boys. He was tried for these allegations and was found to be not guilty.

In 1907 Summers wrote his first book called Aninous and Other Poems that dealt with the subject of pederasty. Summers then converted to Catholicism and he began to tell people he met that he was a Catholic priest. He was not a member of any Catholic church or any diocese at this time. It is still unclear if he was an ordained priest at this time.

Summers was a very intelligent man. He taught both English and Latin at a number of different schools. He gave up teaching to become a full-time writer. He was the founder of the Phoenix which rejected works that he did not feel were up to the standards at the time. He was also elected to the Royal Society of Literature in 1916. Summers studies and wrote on the topic of Gothic Fiction. He wrote a number of short stories and even helped other writers with this topic. A Summer wrote three different anthologies on supernatural subjects and was considered to be the leading writer on the supernatural and gothic fictions by the 1930s.

When it came to religion and his teachings Summers was an usual man. While Summers did attend schooling to be a priest many of his religious writings and his beliefs focused on the occult. His first book on this subject was called The History of Witchcraft and Demonology. He shared his views on what a witch really was and considered witches to be a form of evil. He believed that witches were real and they played a significant role in the Catholic Church. He even made claims that the church knew about the existence of witches but they did not want to share this information with their followers. Summers continued to write about witches and their existence. He stated that the witches were an important part of the church and he even gave suggestions and methods on high to fight back against these witches.

Summers also believed in the existence of vampires. He wrote The Vampire: His kith and Kin as well as The Vampire in Europe. In addition to these creatures, Summers wrote about werewolves and stated that these creatures really existed. While he was a member of the occult his writing style was still considered to be old fashioned at this time. He thought of his subjects as real creatures and wrote in a style that provided information suggesting that they really existed.

Many people even those close to him considered Summers to be a rather odd and mysterious man. He often dressed in clerical wears and his hair was very long. As he aged it turned silver in color. He wore a number of jeweled rings on his hand which is something that men did not really do at that period in time. Some people stated that his physical appearance gave him inspiration when writing his books. People would look at his unusual manners and many stated that helped him get in touch with his characters. For his writing career Summers spend a lot of time doing research. He traveled around looking for information on the supernatural. He also met with others that were in the field of the occult and non mainstream religions and views.

Summers became good friends with Aleister Crowley who was known for studying magic and even developed his own religion in which he was the lead. These men shared a mutual admiration for each other and often shared the information that they have learned in their travels. While they did have opposite views on a number of subjects including religion they would often meet and discuss their practices. Both men knew the occult very well and were able to have respectful disagreements about the topic. It is said that they both learned a lot from these meetings.

Summers was not afraid to make statements that many people did not agree with and was not afraid to explore all areas of history. Through his research, he stated that there were many things in history that other scholars have ignored and information that they did not want to share with the public. He stated that there was a great deal of information that proved the existence of witches, as well as demons and scholars, have chosen to keep this information secret. He studied the information about witchcraft and had to translate books from a number of languages. He then used this information that he found to publish his own books on the subject matter. It did take a long time to cross reference this material but he did get help from leading demonologist at this time. He checked with these scholars to make sure that his information was accurate and factual.

One of the most famous writings that Summers is known for is called Malleus Maleficarum. He translated this book so that the English speaking world could understand the information that it contained. This book was considered to have a great deal of information about how witches were treated. It even contained information on the torture of witches and is a book that is rich in information. When this book was published the only book that outsold it in the entire world was The Bible.

Summers' beliefs went against some of the leaders in the field of witchcraft. He did not think that witches started out with evil intentions. He stated that the very first witches during the Middle Ages just wanted peace and they wanted to be able to be left alone to do their own practices. According to Summers years of persecution and abuse turned witches into evil. At one time there were a real threat to mankind and human survival. Since this time he thought that witches really did turn to a life of evil and their confessions during persecutions were based on fact. He thought that over time witches really did turn into vile creatures.

Witches and other demons were not the only things that Summers would research and write about. He had an interest in the theatre and studied plays and playwrights throughout time. He was the founder of the Shakespeare Head Press and this organization would reprint plays that were written from the 17th century so that they could be used in modern times. These plays also contained a preface that was written by Summers. He also worked as a supervisor for the Production of the Old Plays. This group put on productions of over 18 different plays. They also put on shows of the complete works of William Congrave. Summers even combined his love of the theatre with some of his own research. He produced the play The Witch of Edmonton. It had some realistic elements based on the research that he conducted over the years.

Satan was another topic that Summers was interested in and did a great deal of research on. He accepted that Satan was a real entity and that this entity was very dangers. He believed that Satan sent the witches to Earth to continue his evil deeds.

While Summers' work was not always accepted and many people still do not believe in the creatures that he was writing about his works were often well respected. He was considered to be an interesting man. It was said he was kind, generous, and witty. People that were lucky enough to get close to Summers also reported that he was rather mysterious and they felt that they never really fully knew this man. In his pictures, he was always smiling and was seldom seen to be in a foul mood. He was a very intelligent man and was able to speak to people on a number of different subjects. Even if they did not agree on the matter Summers would listen to the views and the research that other people had conducted. It was hard to tell if he really was a great person or if he was putting on a show. There were even some rumors that in this early year's Summers experimented with black magic. These rumors cannot be confirmed but some people state that is why he was hostile towards witches and vampires. Summers was from a wealthy family and when his father passed he was left a fair amount of money. This allowed him to conduct his research. Summers did make money off of his books and his products as well. Most of the money that he was paid he used for his education and various academic studies. Summers was not originally looking to become famous. People did not begin to take notice of his works until the 1920s. This is when people took notice in his writing and the subjects of witches, vampires, and other demon like creatures. He was considered then to be an expert on this subject matter by others looking to prove their existence. He was an instant influence for those that explored Gothic style writing.

Montague Summers was a respected author even though his subject matter was not popular at the time and many scholars did not take his works all too seriously. They respected his talents but had doubts about the existence of the creatures that he was writing about. Summers died in 1948 at his home.

An autobiography on Summers was published in 1980 but there is still so much that is not known about his life. The grave was unmarked for a number of years until Project Summers was organized. This organization raised funds to get Summers a gravestone. The gravestone states " tell me strange things" which was a saying that Summers was known for.

PARANORMAL INVESTIGATORS 10

SIR WILLIAM CROOKES and FREDERICK BLIGH BOND Jason Conrad Hawes and Grant Steven Wilson

PARANORMAL PIONEERS AND THE MODERN INVESTIGATOR

By.

Rodney C. Cannon & Leo Hardy

CHAPTER ONE SIR WILLIAM CROOKES

Sir William Crookes (17 June 1832 – 4 April 1919)

Sir William Crookes was a British physicist and chemist that attended the Royal College of Chemistry in London. He was a known pioneer of spec-troscopy and vacuum tubes. Crookes invented the tube named after him in 1875. He also invented the Crookes radiometer, a novelty item of sorts today. Beyond the realm of science, Crookes became interested in the paranormal and spiritualism in later life. This change in philosophic journey would even lead to him becoming the president of the Society for Psychical Research in his lifetime.

William Crookes made a career path as a meteorologist, being a profound lecture speaker and teaching multiple courses of study. Crookes worked in the fields of both physics and chemistry. He was noteworthy for his experiments, as they were considered original in their approach and designs. His execution was considered flawless in scientific methods. Crookes was also diverse, with interests that included applied sciences, economics, psychiatric research, and practical mathematics. He was awarded numerous public, academic, and scholastic awards during his life. His honors and achievements in the sciences made him a kind of celebrity personality.

William Crookes was the eldest of 16 children in his family. When appointed to assistant to his teacher in college, he left and embarked on an original path on his own. He studied organic chemistry but found himself more interested in the discovery of new compounds through chemistry. He published several papers concerning the new compound called selenium in the 1850s. While at Radcliffe Observatory in Oxford during 1854, he used wax paper photography to record meteorological parameters with Francis Ronalds, but it was Crookes inventive adaptation. In 1855 he became the appointed lecture speaker for chemistry at the prestigious Chester Diocesan Training College. The next year he married a woman named Ellen Humphrey, having three sons and one daughter with her, being married and living in London.

Over the next few years, Crookes remained devoted to his unique independent work. He formed a publication on science called the Chemical News, being its primary editor and creative spark. It was much less formal than traditional science journals of the day. During this time period, he became fascinated with the early methods of spectral analysis. His first very important discovery would be the element of thallium in the year 1861. He named it after the Greek word thallos because it had a bright green glowing emission line when viewed spectroscopically. With this discovery, his work and reputation became established as a true professional scientist. His election as a fellow member of the Royal Society came quickly after in 1863.

He published a variety of papers about spectroscopy while conducting research on a mix of minor related subjects. His experiments into the conduction of electricity with low-pressure gases led Crookes to discover that as pressure lowered, the cathode seemed to emit rays. Today this is understood that cathode rays are a streaming of free moving electrons, but in Crooke's time his investigations led to his invention of cathode ray tubes. These are used in display devices in modern times, such as televisions and the like. He also was a pioneer in the invention of vacuum tubes and their usage for new studies of physical phenomena. By consequence, he ends up being the first of few scientists that investigated plasma and found it to be a fourth state of matter during 1879. Crookes additionally came up with the idea for the spinthariscope, an instrument used for the study of nuclear radioactivity. It is easy to see that Crooke's experimental science research would become the foundation of discoveries that eventually would change the entire outlook of physics and chemistry in modern science.

Crookes had a younger brother named Philip, who died at age 21 from yellow fever on an expedition throughout Cuba and Florida. This death seemed to have had a profound impact on Crookes because after his brother's death in 1867, he becomes interested in spiritualism. He is said to have attended a séance that year, trying to communicate with his dead brother. From 1871 to 1874, he took time to study under mediums of the day, namely Kate Fox, Daniel D.Home, and Florence Cook. After some time he concluded that mediums were capable of producing genuine psychic phenomena, paranormal communications, and talking with spirits in general. Other skeptical psychologists that new Crookes considered him gullible, as he openly endorsed persons considered to be charlatans of the time. Anthropologist Edward Cloud speculated that since Crookes had bad vision, and despite his honesty, he was short-sighted and could not be trusted for his claims. It is true, that Crookes never got himself spectacles to wear until the 1890s.

In 1875, Crookes invited a medium named Anna Eva Fay to his home to conduct a series of experiments. Fay was a schemer and fraudulent psychic but managed to fool Crookes that she was the real thing. It was the magician Harry Houdini who actually pointed out that Crookes had been deceived. During the coming years, Crookes would continue to propose scientific theories, without much luck. From 1897 to 1906 he proposed that etheric waves explained telepathy, attempted to present theories to prove the legitimacy of spirit photography, and other ideas that he learned in the studies of spiritualism. Professionals in the scientific world debunked and made numerous cases, along with allegations of fraud, conspiracy, and obvious sexual misconduct between Crookes and his various medium female friends. These allegations were proven legitimate on several occasions.

Still Crookes was both a scientist and a spiritualist, without reservations or lack of reasons to be legitimized. In 1900, Crookes becomes an initiate of the Hermetic Order of the Golden Dawn, an offshoot of the O.T.O. formed under Aleister Crowley. In 1895 Crookes discovered helium and was knighted for it two years later. In this same period, he joins the Society for Psychical Research and quickly is made the president, along with joining the Ghost Club and the Theosophical Society. In 1903, Crookes does a series of studies into radioactivity and the radiometer he invents becomes a serious scientific tool. Many things he discovers during this time are relevant to radiation research today. He also remained president of the Society for Psychical Research from 1907 to 1912.

Despite his good and bad reputations in the different lifetime of pursuits he made, Sir William Crookes is a profound and intelligent person in history. Perhaps his open-mindedness for science and the occult is a trait that should be honored, rather than scoffed at. Nonetheless, he was not afraid to follow his heart and mind where they would take him, in his pursuit of truth. Something he did find as much of as he sometimes did not find.

CHAPTER TWO FREDERICK BLIGH BOND

Introducing Frederick Bligh Bond

Frederick Bligh Bond was born on 30 June 1864 and died on 8 March 1945 at the age of eighty. Like many people during his time period, Frederick Bligh Bond had a lot of occupations and specialties. People didn't spend as much time training for their careers back then, and plenty of wealthier people had several jobs throughout their lifetimes.

Frederick Bligh Bond worked as an archaeologist, architect, and illustrator. However, by this point in history, he is primarily known for being a researcher of psychic phenomenon, which was a very popular field at the time.

Early Life and Family

He grew up in a religious family and was born to Reverend Frederick Hookey Bond. Among other things, his father was the Marlborough Royal Free Grammar School headmaster. Frederick Bligh Bond was a home-schooled child and was primarily taught by his headmaster father.

Most people at the time would have known him as Bligh only, in fact, although his name had a lot of connections throughout history. William Bligh, the colonial administrator, was a distant family relation. The novelist, hymn writer, and scholar Sabine Baring-Gould was a cousin of his.

Early Career

Frederick Bligh Bond started out as an architect. Many of the buildings that he designed were schools, interestingly enough. This was during a period of educational reform, and more schools were being constructed in the area in the first place.

He worked as an architect in Bristol from 1888 and onward. He designed the Greenbank Elementary School, the board schools in Barton Hill, Easton, and St. George's School. Modern people will still be able to see his designs on a lot of institutions of higher learning that are still around today.

Frederick Bligh Bond created the Music School of Clifton College and the schools of engineering and medicine at Bristol University. Given the age of most universities, people should be able to appreciate these venerable buildings for years to come.

Some of his commissions as an architect were domestic in nature. They were from the king's Weston estate of Philip Napier Miles. It's possible to see evidence of the architectural work of Frederick Bligh Bond all throughout England, in fact. He managed to do a lot of this work even as he worked as a paranormal investigator. Both career trajectories managed to parallel one another.

Paranormal Investigations

Frederick Bligh Bond became part of the famous Freemasons in the year 1889, so he spent a good portion of his life dedicated to the study of psychic phenomenon. This was only the first of many societies and organizations that he would join in this field, however.

He became part of the Theosophical Society in 1895, joined the famous society for Psychical Research in 1902, was part of the Societas Rosicruciana in Anglia starting in 1909, and he joined the Ghost Club in 1925. As such, there is no doubt that he spent a huge portion of his life in organizations like these, and he had a great deal of experience in that way.

He edited Psychic Science from the year 1921 until the year 1926. It was named the Quarterly Transactions of the British College of Psychic Science at the time, demonstrating the fact that historical titles tended to be less punchy than the ones that people will tend to see today. A lot of the content wasn't all that different.

Frederick Bligh Bond managed to combine a lot of his different fields and studies together. He worked as the director of excavations at Glastonbury

Abbey. Many people today who are interested in psychic archaeology will specifically point to the results that Frederick Bligh Bond got at Glastonbury Abbey.

The retired navy Captain John Allan Bartlett served as a medium when Frederick Bligh Bond tried channeling the spirits of the past at Glastonbury Abbey. Frederick Bligh Bond claimed that he was able to use the method of automatic writing to connect with the dead monks that had lived there.

Perhaps most crucially, Frederick Bligh Bond claimed that he made contact with the long-dead builder of the Edgar Chapel at Glastonbury and that he would never have been able to excavate the area properly otherwise.

Public Reaction

Frederick Bligh Bond managed to build his entire career in the paranormal investigation community off of what happened at Glastonbury Abbey. His 1919 work The Gates of Remembrance was all about it, and he strongly credited his successful excavation of the Glastonbury Abbey with the psychic methods that he used.

However, it was the Church of England who hired him to perform the excavation in the first place. They were not favorable towards spiritualism or to its implications. Going public with his beliefs in paranormal phenomenon strongly cost Frederick Bligh Bond in this way. He was fired in 1921.

These events might have influenced Frederick Bligh Bond's decision to move to the United States in 1926. When he was there, he worked as the education secretary of the American Society for Psychical Research. As such, he was able to find a more welcoming and receptive audience in the United States.

Still, he was not willing to accept all claims about psychic phenomena as being real. Mina Crandon became infamous for faking the evidence of the spirit of her dead brother, Walter. Frederick Bligh Bond certainly did not go against these accusations at any point.

Later Life

Frederick Bligh Bond had an interesting end to his life. He was actually ordained as a priest when he was in the United States, which would probably be shocking to his former employers in the Church of England. He was involved with the Old Catholic Church of America, and he became a bishop in the church in 1933. He went back to the United Kingdom after only about two years and lived there for the rest of his life.

Frederick Bligh Bond had an unusual life in many ways. His life was not entirely what people would expect for a paranormal or supernatural investigator. He demonstrated that people could approach the field from many different vantage points, and he's still remembered for it today.

CHAPTER THREE THE TOOLS OF THE PARANORMAL TRADE

Paranormal investigation, like most occupations, requires a fair amount of knowledge and equipment before one can set out. Unlike the vast majority of occupations, however, ghost hunting and paranormal investigation involve a plethora of mysterious phenomena that cannot always be perceived by the human senses alone and have the potential to be dangerous if not approached with the proper caution and tools.

It should go without saying that the most important thing to have with you during any ghost hunt or investigation is a competent team who will help one another in the unlikely (but entirely possible) event that somebody becomes injured or even possessed. Once the group is assembled, it is imperative that each member equips themselves with the proper supplies. This can be a daunting task, especially for those new to paranormal investigation. With so many new electronics for sale and different advice coming from all directions online, it is often difficult to know where to begin. This chapter will go over everything the modern ghost hunter needs for a safe and successful investigation.

The Basics

Several of the necessary supplies for paranormal investigation are things the average person already has in their home. For instance, a good flashlight is essential, since peak psychic hours are late at night and many popular haunted places lack light sources of their own. It is also important to bring extra batteries, as you never want to be caught in the dark unexpectedly—this can not only leave you vulnerable to any malignant spirits in the area but make accidental injuries unrelated to the paranormal more likely as well. In this same vein, make sure to bring spare chargers and batteries for any electronics you are bringing along, as one never knows exactly how long an investigation will last and a dead camera or cell phone can be the difference between capturing important details and losing them forever.

It is also a good idea to bring a government-issued ID. Ideally, you will have done your research and obtained any necessary permission to enter your desired site during psychic hours, but even so, passersby and sometimes police officers may be alarmed to see you there late at night. This way, you will be equipped to handle these interactions professionally and peacefully. Finally, you should bring a first aid kit, to ensure maximum safety for yourself and your team.

Recording Evidence

One of the most important parts of ghost hunting and paranormal investigation is to document one's findings and capture proof of any paranormal phenomena. There are plenty of tools that can help you do this. For beginners, a simple notebook goes a long way. You can use it to consult your research about the site you are investigating, as well as write down everything from your own thoughts to EMF readings (more on that later). Another helpful tool is an audio recording device you can speak directly into—this way, you can take diligent notes without having to look away from what you are observing.

A camera is also essential. Many paranormal investigators make use of the cameras and audio recorders on their smartphones. However, if this is not possible for you or if you are exploring other options, digital cameras are highly recommended as they can be used to save important evidence directly to your computer (eliminating the risk of losing it). Many digital cameras can also be equipped with infrared capabilities, allowing you to capture clear pictures and footage in very dark settings. No matter what type of camera you choose, be sure to bring a spare charger or plenty of extra batteries or film.

An important tool that is often overlooked is a thermometer. Paranormal energy often coincides with unusual changes in temperature, most often sudden drops. A thermometer will help you identify these and note their exact details.

Electronics

The most important piece of technology for many paranormal investigators is an electromagnetic field (or EMF), reader. These are commonly used by electricians in determining the cause of electrical problems, however, it is well known among the ghost hunting community that abnormal electromagnetic fields, especially moving ones, are strong indicators of the presence of ghosts or spirits. The higher the quality of your EMF reader, the better, as investigators are sometimes confused by EMF readings coming from things such as cell phones and fuse boxes. A clearer reading will help you distinguish the normal from the paranormal. Many higher-end EMF readers also include audio alerts when unusual readings occur, ensuring that investigators do not miss these readings while focusing on other phenomena.

A quality voice recorder is also excellent for picking up EVP, or Electronic Voice Phenomenon. This is a form of paranormal phenomena in which voices that are not picked up by the human ear alone can be heard afterward in electronic recordings. Tape recorders have often been used for this in the past. As with EMF readers, however, voice recorders with more digital capabilities are preferable. EVP often occurs in the midst of heavy static or other background noises. Therefore, you may want to use digital software to minimize other sounds in the recording, making the voices easier to understand.

Another useful tool is a motion sensor. These capture activity that cannot be seen or heard and would otherwise be nearly impossible to document. As with EMF readers, many motion sensors feature audio notifications when something out of the ordinary is detected so that you do not have to monitor them throughout the investigation.

Extras

There are a few things that are not essential to the average ghost hunt or paranormal investigation, but may be useful nonetheless.

A tripod will allow you to keep your video footage steady and spare you and your team from having to carry the video camera throughout the entire investigation. The drawback of using a tripod is that it can be very difficult to record all angles of the room this way. This can be a good tool for stretches of time with low activity, or for teams with more than one video camera. You may also want to try out a Monopod, this is a single leg camera support that many sports photographers have been known to use.

Some investigators also recommend bringing zip ties or another means of restraining a member of your team, in case one of you becomes possessed. However, the chances of this happening are extremely slim and the vast majority of ghost hunts and investigations go smoothly without the need for any restraints.

Also there are now a number of apps available for your smartphone to help the paranormal investigator. Many of the recording devices and even the EMF can be reproduced inside of your iphone. Visit the App store and see what is available.

Lastly, many ghost hunters bring water and snacks along, in order to keep their team alert and hydrated throughout potentially long excursions.

CHAPTER FOUR JASON CONRAD HAWES AND GRANT STEVEN WILSON

When it comes to television shows that go hand in hand with the paranormal world, two television personalities that come to the mind of many of us are Jason Conrad Hawes and Grant Steven Wilson. Due to their first class paranormal programming, they have been able to garner a loyal following around the globe, one that is always attentive to see what these two present to the public. These personalities rose to fame quite quickly with the television reality series Ghost Hunters, which lasted 11 seasons, but their lives reflected paranormal intensiveness way before this program.

The 411 on Jason

Born on December 27, 1971, in Canandaigua, New York, Jason Conrad Hawes begin to see apparitions at the age of 20, and since then, he became fascinated to learn more about anything that deals with the paranormal. Many of his close friends often told him to just let it go, that maybe he was just imagining things, but Mr. Hawes knew that he could not ignore what he was seeing. While others told him to forget about his apparitions, he insisted on finding out more about them. In 1990, he founded the Rhode Island Paranormal Society (RIPS). Three years later, he founded The Atlantic Paranormal Society (TAPS), alongside Grant Steven Wilson.

The 411 on Grant

Grant Steven Wilson was born on July 3, 1974, in Providence, Rhode Island. At the early age of 15, Mr. Wilson had admitted to facing recurring paranormal experiences that were intense in nature, which is the main reason why he and Mr. Hawes ended up meeting. Mr. Wilson offered to redesign the Rhode Island Paranormal website. From there, they became good friends and thus began working on The Atlantic Paranormal Society.

Professional Plumbers

Not only were these two individuals interested in the paranormal, but they were also interested in anything that dealt with plumbing. Being professional plumbers themselves, they worked together for the company Roto-Rooter. They have mentioned that they enjoyed the time they shared with each other in this particular period of their lives.

Ghost Hunters Opportunity Arises

Mr. Hawes and Mr. Wilson proceeded to create the major television hit Ghost Hunters, which was presented in 2004. Ever since it appeared on the Syfy Channel, it became one of the most watched programs on television. The ratings just kept skyrocketing in great numbers; nothing appeared to stop its popularity. They provided the public with a different insight into the paranormal world, by actually going to sites and analyzing anything that appeared to be out of this world. Due to its fame, clips began to be greatly watched on different online platform; therefore, this program began to be shown in many different countries. It was even translated to meet the high demands of the public from other parts of the world.

First Class Equipment Utilized

Throughout this reality series, there were a variety of different instruments that were utilized to be able to help humanity connect with the paranormal, including laptop computers, digital audio recorders, digital video cameras, night vision cameras, thermographic cameras, EMF meters, and even digital thermometers. There have been other reality programs that were and are similar to this one, but what made this one stand out from the rest is that it had a close connection to the public.

Criticism Pours in

Due to the many findings, criticism began to arise. There were people in the media who started to label Ghost Hunters as a fake reality program, one that went the extra mile to make elements appear to be real when in reality they were very far from the truth. Due to the constant allegations that were being made, Jason and Grant had to reassure viewers that the program was 100% authentic. They even went on to mention the details that were stated on the contract they signed before they began to film, which consists that the program had to remain real at all times. The Syfy channel was behind them and made it also clear that what they were stating was factual. Even though the criticism did not seem to subside, it did not hurt the program in any way, as it neither lost sponsorship nor viewers; it remained strong every single season, which is something that cannot be said about other shows that tried to imitate its format, as they fell quite short in almost every aspect.

Their Passion for the Paranormal Continues

Even though the television program Ghost Hunters concluded in late 2016, these two keep informing others about the paranormal world by giving lectures at school and even attending conventions that go hand in hand with this topic that is of high interest to millions of people around the globe. They also participate in a variety of ghost hunting events that are created for paying public at Buffalo Central Terminal in Buffalo, New York, RMS Queen Mary ocean liner in California, and the Stanley Hotel in the beautiful state of Colorado. Their two organizations are still present.

Other Endeavors That They Would Not Change for the World

Besides being still highly interested in the paranormal, these men focus on other areas of life, too. At the moment, Grant is the owner of the board game company Rather Dashing Games, which presents hobby games that are approachable. He has been noted to mention that he really likes to have everything in order in his life, meaning that he does not want to be the type of individual who spends his entire life focused on one single element of life.

On the other hand, Jason has written four thriller screenplays and two books that deal with paranormal activities. This man has always mentioned in the media that he loves helping other people, especially children who are going through health challenges, hence why he makes personal appearances at various social events to raise money for Cure Kids and the Shriners Hospitals for Children.

Only Time Will Tell

Both of these personalities have been offered to host different programs that deal with the paranormal, but at the moment, they are still waiting on the one that is able to grasp their attention the most; therefore, only time will tell when we see them again on the screen, putting us in suspense with every discovery that they make!

CHAPTER FIVE WHY WE CARE ABOUT THE PARANORMAL

-But that the dread of something after death,
      the undiscovered country, from whose bourn
      no traveller returns. - William Shakespeare

When it comes to paranormal research or anything that has something to do with the supernatural, a lot of people tend to scoff, shake their heads, and openly ridicule those individuals who firmly believe that something exists beyond what the naked eye can see. The truth is, paranormal research has been around long enough to prove beyond a shadow of a doubt that things that cannot be explained through traditional science do indeed exist. How else can genuine photographs of spirits, not to mention high-quality EVPs, be explained?

One of the biggest reasons that many people decide to become paranormal researchers is because they have questions of their own that they want answers to. These are genuinely important questions and more often than not, they are many of the same ones that virtually everyone else has. They want to know that there is something more than what is commonly recognized through the five senses that most people use. They want to know that our souls go on after death and that this life in the here and now is not the only thing that exists.

If you really stop and think about it, paranormal research can bring a lot of peace to those individuals who have lost loved ones and want to be reassured that everything about them does not just end. It is comforting to know that loved ones go on to something greater than this existence. The truth is, the belief in an afterlife is something that can bring comfort to many. Again, you can turn to photographs and EVPs to look for proof of the presence of an afterlife. There have been many cases over several decades where this sort of thing has been confirmed again and again.

One question that many people may be asking themselves involves the reasons that more people don't accept this as a fact as opposed to ridiculing those individuals who do know that paranormal research is genuine. Perhaps it has something to do with people's fears. Most individuals have a tendency to ignore the things that truly scare them and for many people, the thought of being able to make contact with the other side is something that is nothing short of terrifying. For others, knowing that they can still talk to their loved ones, who either recently or long ago left this world, brings a comfort that words can simply not describe.

Much of it really comes down to the way that most people have been educated. Some people have issues with paranormal research because of popular culture and the way that it has been portrayed over the years. If you look at movies and television, almost all of the things that focus on anything supernatural center on something negative. Of course, that is not always the case. People that have been around paranormal research know this but others may not. The general public has been trained to think that everything that they experience is going to be like the next horror film or like the myriad of television shows that currently air which always looks at the negative side of the supernatural. As a result, a lot of people don't really want anything to do with the paranormal because they automatically assume that it is going to be exactly like what they have seen. That thought alone terrifies them. Therefore, they don't give it the chance to see what it is really like or what it is really all about.

While this is extremely unfortunate, it is up to the individuals who know better to educate the public. The truth is, there is a lot that still needs to be discovered and as technology increases, knowledge is also increasing along with it. People that seriously research the supernatural are learning more things about the paranormal each and every day.

If you can take only one thing away from this, the most important thing to remember is that everything supernatural does not have to be frightening and that paranormal research is indeed genuine. While there may be people out there that are more interested in producing something that has a shock factor than producing genuine research, there is an equal number of individuals that only focus on serious research which has found some remarkable things in their own right. That is where the focus of paranormal research should actually rest.

Did you love *Paranormal Investigators The Complete Collection Books 1 - 10*? Then you should read *Evil Games That Should Not Be Played* by Leo Hardy!

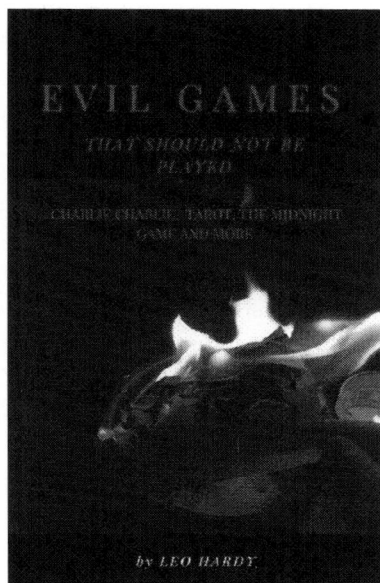

Charlie Charlie, The Hosting Game, Ouija boards, The Midnight Game and a few more are covered in this book.

There are games that have proven to be too dangerous to play and we are not talking about games that involve fast cars, driving, bullets or wild animals, but games that involve the supernatural. Games like **Tarot, Ouija, The Hosting Game** and countless others were contacting spirits have been around for centuries. These games have been causing supernatural infestations for years as well. Despite warnings from those who have played them and members of the clergy people continue to play these games.

In my book **Evil Games That Should not be Played,** you will learn the rules and hazards of some of the most dangerous occult games on earth. The game Charlie Charlie has caused mass hysteria in a group of girls that played it. **One Man Hide and Seek** may be the creepiest game that I have ever researched and countless haunting and satanic incidences can be traced back to the use of spirit and or **Ouija boards.**

Also, you will read about herbs, charms, and talismans used to defend against evil spirits and the cleansing ceremonies that can get rid of them.

I hope that you will read about the games in this book, but I strongly suggest that you play none of them. More than your life may be at risk if you do. You have been warned.

Also by rodney cannon

30 Days Cooking series
Cooking With Strawberries, 30 Days of Cool Recipes

BITTER WATERS SUITE
Bitter Waters Suite, Episode One
Bitter Waters Suite, Episode Two, Reasons to Believe

Empires Falling Short Stories
Hunting The Hand
Empires Falling, The Land of the Khan
The First Port In The Storm
Whispers From A Speaking Demon

microwave cooking
Cooking With Mic, 25 Easy Microwave Recipes and More
Desserts With Mic

PARANORMAL INVESTIGATORS
Paranormal Investigators ed And Lorraine Warren, The Enfield Poltergeist

Paranormal Investigators 2, Amityville An Ed and Lorraine Warren File
Paranormal Investigators 3 The Exorcist, Father Gabriele Amoth
Paranormal Investigators The Collection Books 6 - 10
Paranormal Investigators The Complete Collection Books 1 - 10

The serial killers
The Serial Killers, Pure Evil
The Serial Killers The Sadistic Seven
The Serial Killers, The Female Serial Killers
The Serial Killers, Butchers and Lunatics
The Serial Killers Collection

Standalone
On Writing A Low Budget Screenplay
Running An Online Business, Ending the Confusion
On Low Budget Film Making,Digital Film Making Interviews
Calling Vicki
On Making A Found Footage Film
The Micro Budget Film Making Collection
Cooking With Ketchup, 30 Go To Recipes
Microwave Cooking, The Microwave cookbook Collection

Watch for more at cannondigitalfeaturefilmmaking.blogspot.com.

Printed in Great Britain
by Amazon